Simon Tugwell OP

Prayer:

Living with God

Templegate Publishers
Springfield, Illinois 62705

Published by arrangement with

Veritas Publications
Dublin, Ireland

© 1975 Simon Tugwell

Published in the United States of America by
Templegate Publishers
302 East Adams Street
P.O. Box 5152
Springfield, Illinois
62705-5152

ISBN 0-87243-100-2

Acknowledgements

The author and publishers are obliged to the following:
Faber and Faber for quotations from Don Marquis *The Lesson of the
Moth*. Oxford University Press for a quotation from C.S. Lewis *Letters
to Malcolm*. The Division of Christian Education of the National Council
of Churches for quotations from the R.S.V. Bible. W.P. Watt and Son
for quotations from the Grail Psalter. Charles E. Tuttle and Co. for a
quotation from *Zen Flesh, Zen Bones*.

Contents

Introduction

"Prayer," according to one ancient definition, "is keeping company with God."[1] And that really throws us right in at the deep end. Prayer is not another part for us to act, another skill for us to master, another subject to study for an examination : it is a relationship, and a relationship with God. And even in this age of computerised dating, one can only learn to keep company with someone by keeping company with them and accepting the consequences. Any relationship except the most superficial affects and changes us; it challenges us to respect the freedom, the mystery, the otherness of the other, and, perhaps even more disturbing, it will sooner or later bring to light our own freedom, the mystery of ourselves, the unknownness and unpredictability of ourselves. How we respond to such a challenge, to such a bringing to light, will in very large measure decide whether we grow and mature in life, or whether we shrivel up. And it is surely a fact that, while some people are genuinely afraid of the dark, all of us are rather afraid of the light. As the archbishop says in T. S. Eliot's play, *Murder in the Cathedral*, "Human kind cannot bear very much reality".[2]

Yet God is truth and his light is infinite. To keep company with him allows finally of no hankering after darkness, after that safe world of blurred edges and comfortable anonymity. We who have been baptised into the death of Jesus have been taken out of darkness and brought into the light; we have been named. It does not matter very much if, for the moment, our eyes are dazzled, our brains reeling and bewildered, and our hearts thumping with terror. The question is : will we turn and bolt? Or will we give it a try, and make the attempt to be children of the light? If we choose to give it a try, then we have already embarked on the adventure of keeping company with God, the adventure of true prayer.

I say quite advisedly that we have already embarked on this adventure. G. K. Chesterton, with his usual wit, makes fun of the man who "criticises this world as if he were house-hunting . . . No man is in that position. A man belongs to this world before he begins to ask if it is nice to belong to it. He has fought for the flag, and often won heroic victories for the flag long before he has ever enlisted".[3]

There is something not unlike this to be said about being a Christian. Especially in this age when we hear so much about commitment and free decision, we must be reminded that our Lord said quite categorically : "You have not chosen me, I have chosen you" (Jn 15:16). There is a very true sense in which we must say that no one can ever choose to become a Christian, any more than anyone can

baptise himself. The basic ritual symbol in the rite
of baptism is, after all, being ducked, and you cannot duck yourself! St Paul did not choose to be
overwhelmed by the revelation of the light of Christ;
he was thrown in the deep end. Only then does
choosing come in: when you discover yourself in the
deep end, you have to react in some way; and on
that reaction will depend what comes of it.

"Prayer," according to a Byzantine spiritual
writer,[4] is "the manifestation of baptism". If this is
true, we should expect it to reflect the essential char-
acteristics of baptism. And sure enough, we find an
emphatic tradition especially among Eastern Christians that prayer is not something that we can
originate, precisely because it is already going on.
The Holy Spirit is praying within us; there is a
prayer in the heart of every man.[5]

.   .   .   .

It is no doubt true, in absolute theological terms,
to say that, by virtue of the Incarnation of the Son
of God, all mankind is already in the deep end. But
until, in one way or another, we actually discover
that we are in the deep end, there really is very little
one can do about it.

Two of the parables that our Lord told about
the kingdom of God illustrate this very well. First:
"The kingdom of God is like a man throwing seed
on the ground, and he sleeps and gets up again,
night and day, and the seed springs up and grows,
he does not know how; the earth brings forth of its

own accord" *(Mk 4:26–28)*. Taken in conjunction with the preceding parable of the sower, this does suggest one practical question, but only one: how can we be good soil, so that the seed sown in us will really get a chance to grow and bring forth a good crop? The rest of the process would seem to be right outside our choosing.

Secondly: "The kingdom of heaven is like treasure hidden in a field. A man finds it . . ." *(Mt 13:44)*. All kinds of decisions have to be made once the treasure is found. But you cannot decide to find it in the first place; you just stumble upon it, as it were, when going for your afternoon walk. Again, the only practical choice open to us would seem to be the choice to go for afternoon walks, not always to stay safely at home; and to keep our eyes open.

Our Lord's directive to the apostles before his Ascension is that they are to "sit in Jerusalem", to sit and wait until the Holy Spirit comes *(Lk 24:49)*. And there is no reason to believe that they had any inkling in advance of what that would mean—after all, they were still looking for the messianic kingdom to be realised politically *(cf. Acts 1:6)*.

So when our Lord tells us to seek, to knock, to ask *(Mt 7:7)*, that is not the first directive. We begin to seek, when we have in a more or less accidental way (accidental at least as far as we are concerned) found some kind of clue. We knock when we have found some kind of door. We ask when we have got some idea of what to ask.

It is always God who calls men to keep company with him, never the other way about. His call may indeed sometimes come to us in the form of a desire for prayer and contemplation; but we shall not have got very far before he makes it clear that the initiative is still and always in his hands.

. . . .

And so this book is addressed chiefly to anyone who, like me, finds himself unaccountably thrown in the deep end, splashing and struggling and hoping that it will turn out to be "swim" rather than "sink", though sometimes rather suspecting that it is going to be "sink". Should he find the time to stop and think about it, he will be embarrassingly aware that to a spectator safe on dry ground, his antics will look utterly clownish and unintelligible, but there is nothing that can be done about that. We can only hope that our very foolishness and help-lessness will draw the God of mercy to our assistance.

This book is concerned with our relationship with God in general. It tries to suggest some of the basic factors involved in becoming the kind of people who can keep company with God and, more importantly, *enjoy* his company. I am deeply conscious that it represents only one possible ap-proach, one possible way of constellating Christian attitudes and pastimes. Things that are central and pivotal to me may appear, and indeed may be, peripheral in the lives of others; and it is more than likely that many readers will be dismayed that I appear indifferent to things which stir their deepest devotion.

A good monk once told me that he thought every Christian has his special text, round which everything else will sooner or later fall into place. There are many, many different points of condensation for the Christian life. I do not offer these reflections of mine in any spirit of competition with other, excellent books that are available, with their many different approaches to prayer. The Jews came to believe that the manna in the desert tasted to each man of his own favourite food *(Wis 16:21)*; in the same way, he who is the one, unique Way is rich enough to be many ways to suit the different needs and temperaments of men. My hope and my prayer is simply that all who read this book will find that it speaks to them of God, so that they may all go on their own ways with renewed joy and confidence.

Few of the ideas in this book are original, but it would be impossible for me to say just where they all came from. I thank God for the many people who have helped and inspired me, and whose prayers have supported me.

In particular I must express my unbounded gratitude to the Daughters of the Cross, who permitted me to use the occasion of preaching their retreat to build up the material for this book, and who, in addition, most generously transcribed all the talks that I gave them. Without the help of this raw material, the book would simply not have been written.

Finally, I must thank my brethren for their various assistance, and especially those who kindly gave their time up to read and comment on the different drafts of the book. To them I dedicate this work, with gratitude and affection.

Prayer:
Living with God

Weakness of faith combined with strength of intellect
is apt to lead to the error of talkativeness.

Tibetan Precepts of the Gurus.[6]

I am a fool, and I cannot bear to keep secret
how wonderful God is.

St Barsanuphius [7]

1 Remembering God

Forgetfulness is the root of all evil
An unknown Egyptian monk[8]

In our relationship with God, one of the main problems is that half the time we just forget about it. We may have the most beautiful and edifying thoughts during our morning prayers, and whole new vistas of Christian life may from time to time open out before us, but yet when it actually comes to the practical crunch, it just seems to slip right out of our minds. And at the end of the day we kick ourselves for having been just as unforgiving, uninspiring, unregenerate, as ever.

The medieval theologians tell us that we must build up habits of virtue, getting used to behaving in a Christian way, so that we shall eventually be able spontaneously to react to things in a way expressive of Gospel truth. And of course this is true. Christianity is not unlike learning to drive. There is a place for learning the book of rules off by heart; and it is a sign of progress to be able to change gear at all, even with much time and thought. But we are not really able to drive until we can be pretty sure that we shall be able to react spontaneously and

3

appropriately to the unforeseen circumstances of the road. It must become second nature to us to behave, to react, in a certain way, as drivers—and as Christians.

All this is true. But habits must begin somewhere. And just where we need to build up good habits is often precisely the occasion where we simply forget all about it. For all our beautiful meditations on forgiveness, when someone actually treads on our toe, we hit him; and only remember afterwards that we were supposed to turn the other toe over to him too.

Somehow we must find a way of remembering God that does not work in fits and starts, but that will actually last through the day; a kind of fundamental remembrance of God that will affect our heart, and allow our most unpremeditated and spontaneous behaviour to be transformed, as it were, at the root.

And this is, in fact, what meditation is supposed to achieve. It is not primarily a matter of spending a certain period of time every now and then having beautiful thoughts, but about building up a Christian memory. In fact, some traditional methods of meditation were originally mnemonic devices having nothing to do with religion.[9]

Building up a Christian memory will unavoidably take time. It is a big mistake to look always for immediate results; and to insist always on drawing some immediately applicable moral from one's meditation may actually frustrate the whole operation.

Learning to drive a car involves learning to do a lot of things that will probably have no immediate use; it is to a large extent building up reserves, acquiring a kind of memory that will enable one to deal speedily with whatever emergencies may arise. A Christian needs to have a Christian memory to allow him to deal with the unforeseen circumstances of his road too. Meditation can be seen as a kind of rehearsal for the unknown future; and the more diverse the material one has stored away in one's reserves, the better prepared one will be.

And in fact "rehearse" is the basic meaning of the Latin word from which we get our word "meditation". A Latin classic well known to those who still read such things introduces us to a shepherd boy "meditating" on his flute.[10] And this reminds us that the basic meaning of "rehearse" is to rehearse one's lines. A Hebrew word in the Old Testament usually translated "meditate" originally has vocal connotations, meaning to growl or to mutter (e.g. Ps 1:2; 36:30, os iusti meditabitur sapientiam).

A very traditional first stage in meditation, in building up a Christian memory, is in fact simply to recite all or parts of the Bible, until one has it more or less off by heart.[11] Mere memorising of the catechism is out of favour these days, but there was a very sound principle and a long tradition behind it. It may even go back to our Lord himself.[12] Christians from very long ago used to recite the creed on all possible occasions, and a similar practice goes right back into the Old Testament: "You shall lay up these words of mine in your heart and in your soul, and you shall bind them as a sign on your hand and they shall be as frontlets between your eyes, and you shall teach them to your children, talking of them when you are sitting in your house and when you are walking by the way, and when you lie down and when you rise"*(Deut 11:18–19)*.

The basic point is that we need to be familiar with more doctrine than we actually require for immediate use, so that we will be prepared for whatever emergencies may arise; and the emergencies in this case are not just the hazards of life, but also the graces given to us by God, which we shall often be unable even to recognise, let alone respond to, if we have not got the reserves of doctrine to light them up.

So we need reserves, and that is the point of knowing one's doctrine, knowing one's Bible, knowing the lives and writings of the saints and the great theologians of the Church. How we acquire this material will, of course, depend on our temperament, education, and many other factors; some may get it more through reading, others through visual art forms, others through hearing sermons, lectures, wireless programmes. Some may easily memorise a lot of the Bible, others may know only a bit. It is not absolute quantity that matters, only that there should be enough variety to provide for a certain amount of flexibility of response. A driver who knows only how to turn left will not get very far! The basic essentials of doctrine have been crystallised out in the creeds; and the new liturgy gives us a fairly rich diet of scripture. It is to be hoped that Church music will also increase our stock.

The chief caution that must be mentioned here is that we must do our best not to censor our input except where censorship is due. And it is not due in our reading of the Bible. To call the various books of the Bible "Bible", "sacred scripture", "inspired", means essentially the very practical matter of the way we use them: that we trust them to speak to us with the voice of God, and therefore do not systematically exclude any part of them from our use. That is not to say that we must try actually to use the whole Bible; that must depend on a lot of human factors. But we must not censor it, we must not deliberately exclude the bits that do not appeal to us or make sense to us. We must let them be there, as part of our stock.

Nor is it our business to censor Church doctrine. In an age which is so conscious of the virtue of being a good listener, it is curious how little attention is paid to the virtue of being a good listener to the voice of the Church; by which I do not mean only or even primarily the magisterium of the Church, though that is certainly not excluded, but the voice of tradition, of all our fellow Christians down the ages, stumbling and fumbling, but yet constantly returning to certain basic points, which become all the more solid and decisive for being reached from so many different angles. Being a good listener means, at the very least, being able to suspend judg-

ment, to let someone have his say, without jumping
to conclusions after the first word has been uttered.

And this brings me to a very important point
about what we may call "digesting" our input. We
must not be in too much of a hurry to understand;
or at any rate we must be very tentative and experi-
mental in our understanding. Think of St Peter at
his most glorious moment, when he has confessed
Jesus as Messiah, and is assured that this came to
him from God's own inspiration; he is solemnly
declared to be the Rock upon which the Church is
to be built. But he presumes on his understanding,
and tries to divert our Lord from the appointed
course of his passion. This is no heavenly revelation,
it is from Satan the enemy. How dangerous it is to
understand! *(Mt 16, 13ff)*.

We must remember that the first original sin, as
it is depicted in the Bible, is a sin of knowledge mis-
appropriated. Our minds are certainly meant to be
involved in the Gospel, and we are told to love God
with all our mind as well as our heart and soul
(Mt 22:37). We must not be afraid of having minds.
But we must be aware that our minds are at least
as capable of running away with us as our legs or
our emotions are. There is an understanding that
comes from the Holy Spirit, but there is also an
understanding which shuts out the Holy Spirit.

What we must beware of is the kind of understanding that disposes of everything. The man who
knows all the answers is likely to be a bore, even to
himself. His world is dead. If we read the Bible with

a view to pinning every text down to a precise
doctrinal or experiential significance, we shall end
up with a book full of dead letters. If we seek an
exhaustive interpretation of every point of doctrine,
in terms of some system of thought, we shall end up
with yet more dead letters. According to St Thomas
Aquinas[13] the object of faith, strictly speaking, is
the reality underlying the scriptural and dogmatic
formulae; we must reach through the words to the
living reality, which can never be contained in any
understanding. Our friends, after all, become more
mysterious the better we know them. How much
more will God escape our final comprehension!

But precisely because of this living elusiveness,
the words are terribly important. St Thomas, for all
his insistence on the reality behind the words, nevertheless insists with equal firmness that we cannot
bypass the words. And this is because the words too
are living words, which in their own way resist and
challenge our narrowing interpretations just as much
as does the living reality of God himself. In fact, the
recalcitrance of the words is a sacramental means by
which the transcendence of God is made present to
us.

Just as the words of good poetry are never
exhausted by any number of commentaries, and can
never be adequately paraphrased in prose, just as it
is quite different to be told the gist of a story from
actually reading it in its entirety, so the words of
scripture and the formulae of dogma are never
exhausted by any understanding we may have of

them. And their inexhaustibility symbolises and mediates the livingness of the divine reality.

We must be prepared, then, to listen and to learn, without being too quick to understand. We must allow the various elements to come together in different, often very fleeting, though suggestive, ways, to illumine the scenery of our lives; not in a dull fluorescent way, but with something of the romance of firelight, and something of the inadequacy of candlelight which leaves you in the dark where you wanted light, but then unexpectedly highlights something you have never noticed before; and, of course, something of the terror of lightning.

In fact, it is interesting that in the past Christians used the Bible in a way not unlike one of the procedures used by modern psychiatrists. One way of finding out what a person is really like, is to shoot words at him, and tell him to reply with the first word that comes into his head; such random associations of words, uncontrolled by deliberate thought or reflection, can tell an expert a lot about what a person really is, because it undercuts or by-passes all the normal ways in which we present ourselves, and does not allow us to don a pleasing mask, to show ourselves as we would like to be, as we would want to be thought to be, maybe even think we are.

We can use the Bible in the same kind of way. As more and more of it sinks into our memory, it is more and more likely that any passage we read will spark off a whole chain of associations, some of them from other parts of the Bible, some of them drawn from the stuff of our life. For instance, a word in the passage we are reading may remind us of a totally different passage where the same word occurs; maybe the connexion is only by way of a pun, but punning is a very basic human activity, featuring even in our dreams. Provided there is not too much deliberate control, we may find ourselves getting tremendously involved, not in scientific exegesis, but in a living relationship with the living Word. It may convict us, humble us, excite us, challenge us, move us to tears of joy or despair or contrition . . . the important thing is that it should get into us, get under our skin; and that it should engage us at a level deeper than that of our own deliberate choice.

After all, God's word is addressed to us as we really are, not as we like to present ourselves; he speaks to our heart, not to our mask. It is not only that little bit of us which we have, as it were, colonised and made subject to our control, that is involved in the Christian enterprise: it is the whole man.

Just as the psychiatrists use random association to bring to light the true nature of their patient's problems, so we should allow the Bible to bring us into the light, the light of God's truth. God is not taken in by our polite little speeches. He knows us through and through, far better than we know ourselves. He hears what we are really saying, he listens to our heart. And if we would learn to keep company with him, we must become the kind of people who are prepared to be heard and addressed at that deep level, which requires a great deal of honesty and humility.

Then the Lord can really get hold of us, below the level of our deliberate control. He can get us hooked—he is, after all, a fisherman—so that, even though we may kick and scream and try to get away, he will at the end be able to land us safely at his feet.

As long as our religion remains at the level of our deliberate, not to say contrived, personality, it is bound to be a rather on-and-off affair; if we allow the Lord to get hold of us at the level of what the Bible calls the heart, below the level of contrivance, then we have a traitor in the camp! We shall become involved with God even in spite of ourselves, there will be something in us undermining our self-built edifice of conceit and self-will, so that it will not be quite so easy for us to go on forgetting God and his commands and promises at every critical moment. Our very spontaneity will begin to be transformed at its roots. A seed of the kingdom will have been sown in the deep soil of our being. And "the earth brings forth of its own accord". Whether we like it or not, a harvest of Gospel values will begin to spring up. We shall be faced with the challenge and the opportunity to grow up in the Lord.

Our Lord knows very well that we cannot take very much of the Gospel at once; but he also knows that, left to ourselves, we should conveniently omit all the tricky bits. So his provision for his people is very precise and well-designed to fit our situation. First of all, he tells us all kinds of things, knowing very well that it is not going in. Then he sends the Holy Spirit to us, with the assurance that "he will remind you of all that I have said to you" *(Jn 14:26)*. Surely this is a very essential working of the Holy Spirit in our lives. In our reading, memorising and meditation we accumulate the materials, we hear the Lord's teaching. But then it must be picked out and applied to actual situations in our lives, and this is what the Holy Spirit does. He reminds us of what we have already learned in principle, just at the time that we need to know it.

Maybe we have gone through life happily quarrelling with those who quarrel with us, giving as good as we got if not better. And then, one fine day, the Holy Spirit decides to intervene. Just when you are about to set off on a tremendous rampage, out of the blue comes the thought: "Love your enemies; pray for those who persecute you". And you have to make a choice. You can, of course, go on with your rampage if you want to; but only at the expense of refusing a specific grace of God.

As long as we only remembered afterwards that we were supposed to forgive, there was no problem: we could have our rampage and then go to confession. But when the Holy Spirit calls things to mind, pointing them out, sometimes very pointedly, just at—from our unregenerate point of view—the very worst possible time, then we have to make a real choice: do we accept the offer, the new possibility opened out before us by the inscrutable working of God's grace, or do we refuse, which is a far more serious and damaging thing than merely forgetting?

If we want to keep company with God, we must be prepared to let him remind us of his ways, not at the times that suit us, but at the times that suit him. If, through our use of the Bible, through our reading and meditation, we let him into our hearts, below the level of our deliberation, that means that we hand over to him the right to choose how and when to present himself to our consciousness. We all like keeping God in a cupboard with the best china and the family silver, to look at when we feel inclined. But the living God chooses his own times, and will come when he is not wanted.

True scripture reading, then, true attention to doctrine, true meditation, involves a surrender of our independence, a letting go of our right always to be the one to choose. It will not necessarily lead to the kind of moral or spiritual improvement that would satisfy our vanity; it will not eliminate, therefore, the whole problem of forgetfulness: we shall still often forget, when we would have liked to remember the words of the Gospel and our own good resolutions. But the stronghold of our self-centredness will have been breached. We may not always remember what and when *we* will; but *we* shall be reminded, forcibly and with the full judgment of God behind it, by the Holy Spirit calling things to mind when they are actually needed, with sublime disregard for our superficial comfort or convenience.

If we will learn to listen, to listen deeply to the Word of God, we shall sooner or later have to realise that it is the Word of him who is truly Lord, and whose sovereign freedom is not bounded by our decisions.

2 Space to Pray in

I'd rather learn from one bird how to sing than teach ten thousand stars how not to dance.

whenever men are right they are not young.

e. e. cummings[14]

It would be nice if our forgetfulness of God arose simply from sheer absent-mindedness; but unfortunately it does not. There are positive obstacles in the way of our remembering God, and these must be faced squarely and sensibly.

One very serious obstacle is constituted by what we may call imaginational cramp. We may attend faithfully to our input in the way of reading the Bible and getting to grips with doctrine, without it ever really bearing much fruit, because our picture of God and of the Christian life, and perhaps of everything, is too rigid or prickly to allow for much growth.

The Bible talks quite frequently about the need for our eyes to be opened; many of our Lord's miracles are concerned precisely with restoring sight to those born blind, and they have traditionally been taken as symbolic also of his opening the eyes of our heart, to make us capable of deeper vision. And the ancient theologians were reluctant to make too sharp a distinction between our capacity for spiritual vision in the strict sense, and our capacity for any kind of vision. If we want to see God, we must learn to see.

One part of this is that we must have mental images and pictures that are conducive to vision, and here we are often sadly ill-equipped. All too often we are effectively blinded by having a wrong picture of life.

The problem is not just that of simple blindness, but that, being blind, we think we can see; it is something like that appalling condition indicated by our Lord when he said, "If the very light that is in you is darkness, then what darkness!" *(Mt 6:23;* cf. *Jn 9:41).* Our eyes were opened, in one sense, just as the serpent promised, when Adam and Eve ate the forbidden fruit *(Gen 3:5).* It is the blindness of false vision that must be healed by Christ.

One kind of blindness is indicated when he said to the Jews, "How can you believe, while you accept glory from one another?" *(Jn 5:44).* We can be blinded by our fear of being ostracised or regarded as eccentric. Human respect can easily hold us back not just from action but even from seeing. We need to foster in ourselves a view of life that does not drive us to go always with the crowd, but that lets us see also the possibility that the crowd may be wrong. "The gate is wide and the way is spacious that leads to destruction and there are many who go that way; but it is a narrow gate and a hard way

that leads to life, and they are few who find it"
(Mt 7:13-14). This does not entitle us to consign
most of our fellow men to Hell, but it does oblige us
to recognise that the majority is not necessarily right.
We shall not be saved simply by following the fashion.
One of the purposes of studying history and of
science fiction and fantasy literature is to reduce the
overwhelmingness of the particular crowd that sur-
rounds us, so that we can begin to suspect that the
crowd itself may only be an odd one out, when
viewed from some larger perspective. So we can be
freed from the tyranny of "things present" and from
the obligation of contemporaneity *(cf. Rom 8:38;
Gal 1:4)*.

Another kind of blindness is brought out vividly
by the once famous medieval Dominican, William
Peraldus:[15] men who are too keen on money "have
their eyes in their purse instead of in their head". If
the world is viewed only in terms of the cash-register,
we shall not see very much. We shall certainly be
unlikely to see God walking in the garden in the
cool of the evening. We need sufficient imaginative
space to be able to ask what the true, unfinancial
value of money is; maybe even to ask what the
value of value is.

Another way of being blind is to see the world
only as a problem, as a challenge to us to do something about it, or to organise something, even if it is
only a coach to bring other people to see it, or to
write it up in the local paper. It is perhaps to help us
overcome this kind of visional cramp that philoso-

phers have sometimes wondered what happens to things when we are not looking at them. In their film, *The Yellow Submarine,* the Beatles imagined a corridor in which a whole menagerie of improbable people and creatures came out to disport themselves whenever no one was looking. Do you know what goes on outside your door when you have shut it?

The world is not just there for us to do things to it. It is just there. And so are we, as part of that world. It is good for us sometimes to be stared at by an indifferent blackbird or coldshouldered by a cat. After all, what are we to them? How can we ever find out what we are to them? We are not the centre of the world!

But perhaps the worst kind of blindness is that which occurs when we simply take everything for granted, so that there is no room in our world for surprise, for wonder, for appreciation. That is the real death of seeing, because when we "know it all already", we have no need to look. The common saying, "Seeing is believing" is all too horribly true in such a case : blind faith in the monotonous sameness of all things actually replaces seeing.

One factor in this kind of blindness is an exaggerated use of a mechanistic model, applied to everything without distinction. For instance, in a machine, if one part suddenly starts behaving in an idiosyncratic and unprogrammed way, the only result is that the machine goes wrong, it breaks down. But such a model has only very limited applicability to human or even vegetable society. When someone steps out of

B

line, mankind may be impoverished, certainly, or inconvenienced, but except in extremely improbable circumstances cannot be said meaningfully to "break down". A marriage is more likely to break down from an excess of programming than from a lack of it. A student who does not simply follow the course prescribed for him may produce brilliant and original insights; and the technologist who makes machines may revolutionise the world by taking time off from finding new answers to the same old questions, and indulging in a little daydreaming in which new questions may arise.

Again, our boredom with life is surely due at least in part to the utterly misleading acceptance of mass production as the norm for sameness and repetition. There indeed things are bound to soulless repetition. But why should we suppose that the sun is *bound* to rise again, day by day? All that we observe is that it does rise day by day. Maybe Chesterton's interpretation is far more just, that the sun rises over and over again because God is enjoying it so much. Every time is "positively the last appearance", but the audience will not let it go.[16]

We need imaginative models, ways of looking at life, that leave room for novelty, for amazement, for that hesitant, enquiring joy that comes when we think we recognise something but are not quite sure . . . And this might help us to rediscover how surprising, in fact, even the everyday things are too.

In a rather mediocre poem on poetry, Emily Dickinson says:

> This was a Poet—It is That
> Distills amazing sense
> From ordinary Meanings—
> And Attar so immense
>
> From the familiar species
> That perished by the Door—
> We wonder it was not Ourselves
> Arrested it—before—
> Of Pictures, the Discloser . . .[17]

Our use of the imagination, and not just our visual imagination but all the ways we form and use pictures of the world, should be such as to give us space to see and appreciate the "familiar species", the things we take for granted, the stuff of ordinary life.

As so often, G. K. Chesterton exactly catches the point, in a chapter of *Orthodoxy* which is a splendid antidote to imaginational cramp : "Nursery tales say that apples were golden only to refresh the forgotten moment when we found that they were green. They make rivers run with wine only to make us remember, for one wild moment, that they run with water".[18]

It is interesting that St Augustine makes an identical point about miracles in his discussion of the miracle at Cana.[19] "Our Lord's miracle in turning water into wine comes as no surprise to those who know that it is God who did it. At the wedding that day he made wine in the six waterpots he had had filled with water; but he does the same thing every year in the vines. The servants put the water in the jugs, and he turned it into wine. In just the same way

the Lord turns into wine the water that the clouds
drop. Only that does not amaze us, because it happens
every year . . . So the Lord kept back certain unusual
things for himself to do, to wake us up with miracles
to worship him."

The miracle that breaks the rules reminds us that
the rules themselves are miraculous. We need to rediscover and to cherish a basic sense of wonder, of
surprise, of the precariousness of actuality. Ecclesiastes, the dismal world-weary preacher of the Old
Testament, might grumble that "there is nothing
new under the sun" *(Eccles 1:9)*; but the New
Testament answers loudly and excitedly, "Look! I
am making all things new" *(Apoc 21:5)*. Of course
we may all of us sometimes get Ecclesiastes moods,
and if we do, it is comforting to know that they are
not utterly debarred from God's domain; but we
should not devote our minds and imaginations to
prolonging and justifying them. We should aim
rather to have minds and imaginations able to respond joyfully to the truth that in Christ everything
is given back its youth and at least something of the
freshness of the very first days of creation.

> Morning has broken
> Like the first morning,
> Blackbird has spoken
> Like the first bird.
> Praise for the singing!
> Praise for the morning!
> Praise for them, springing
> Fresh from the Word![20]

To experience the world like this must lead us,
however indefinitely, in the direction of prayer, because this kind of appreciation cannot help but in-
clude an element of thanksgiving. As Chesterton
said: "Children are grateful when Santa Claus puts
in their stockings gifts of toys or sweets. Could I not
be grateful to Santa Claus when he put in my stockings the gift of two miraculous legs?"[21]

We need not be shy of these very simple expres-
sions of natural religious sentiment: they are the
foundation for more supernatural religion. But if they
do not meet with suitable images and symbols in our
faith, then they will either atrophy or seek fulfilment
elsewhere, and either way our faith will be impoverished and inhibited from really taking root in our
hearts. It was surely an inadequate picture of God
that left Milton's imagination and sympathy inevitably drawn to the side of Satan, as has often been
remarked. Other, less disciplined, souls have actually
resorted to Satanism in the attempt to satisfy their
innate religious needs.

In the past 70 or 80 years there has been a
healthy rediscovery of symbolic theology, reminding
us of the imaginative richness there is in the Bible
and in our ancient texts. The austere language of
classical metaphysics has its place, but should never
have been allowed to claim monopoly.

In fact, there is a most important principle which
we find stated most clearly by that great and difficult
mystic who wrote under the name of Dionysius the
Areopagite.[22] He asks why the Bible uses such seem-

ingly inappropriate and irreverent images of God and
of heavenly realities. His answer is that this is actually
one of the best safeguards against idolatry. To call
God good or light or perfection is just as metaphori-
cal as to call him a rock or an unjust judge or
(implicitly) a bed, all of which we find in the Bible;
but we are more likely to be taken in by the respectable images and mistake them for literal truth, and
so confine God within the limits of our own concepts,
which is, of course, idolatry. Would that the former
Bishop of Woolwich had heeded that warning before
telling a startled England that its image of God had
to go! The high-sounding metaphysical language that
he bids us use is actually far more likely to deceive
us than any number of old men with white beards
sitting on thrones in the sky. C. S. Lewis makes the
point well: "Never let us think that while anthropo-
morphic images are a concession to our weakness, the
abstractions are the literal truth. Both are equally
concessions; each singly misleading, and the two
together mutually corrective. Unless you sit to it very
lightly, continually murmuring, 'Not thus, not thus,
neither is this Thou', the abstraction is fatal. It will
make the life of lives inanimate and the love of loves
impersonal. The naïf image is mischievous chiefly in
so far as it holds unbelievers back from conversion.
It does believers, even at its crudest, no harm".[23]

Not only must we not be duped by respectable
abstractions; we must not be duped by respectable
pictures and images either. As a child, I used to own
an antique Book of Common Prayer endowed, among

other delights, with a picture of Guy Fawkes sneaking
into the Houses of Parliament to blow them up. In
the top right hand corner of the picture was an
enormous eye watching him. The image is all too
familiar, isn't it? God is that all-seeing eye, the ever-
present policeman, constantly prying into all our
misdeeds. And that is, of course, one picture the
Bible does contain, though generally in a less vindic-
tive context.

But the Bible also shows us God as being himself
a burglar *(Mt 12:29)*. And that turns our whole
imaginative space upside down and inside out.

So long as our view of the Christian life is
dominated by the thought that we are constantly
exposed to the gaze of a somewhat exacting potentate,
with strict rules, both moral and ceremonial, for his
courtiers, then obviously it must appear that the
Gospel appeals primarily to our conformist instincts.

But St Paul says: "Do not be conformed to this
world" *(Rom 12:2)*. Perhaps the primary appeal is
not to our conformist, but to our non-conformist
instincts? Perhaps we have fought too shy of the
apparently less respectable images we find in the
Bible and in the theologians and spiritual writers of
the Church, and so have been duped by the respectable ones, and have been partially or completely
crippled by it?

St Ephrem the Syrian, in one of his hymns, says:
"The Evil one went mad when he saw that young
men ran to Saba (a famous monk) in the desert, that
they *misbehaved* and abandoned worldly desires and

learned chastity in the monastic habitations".[24] The word rendered "misbehaved" is used in Syriac especially of people being unfaithful to their wives. God is inciting us to "misbehave", to be unfaithful to our first love and forsake the snake who wooed and wedded us.

He is also inciting us to run away from our duties. St Theodore the Studite, the great monastic reformer, calls his monks "runaway slaves";[25] and Clement of Alexandria speaks of all Christians as "deserters" : "It is a beautiful adventure to desert to God".[26] This is, after all, a very precise interpretation of one of the first acts in the baptismal liturgy, the act of "dropping out of line" *(apotaxis)*, abandoning the devil's camp for that of God.

Before we settle down too sedately to the thought that "God is not a God of confusion" *(1 Cor 14:33)*, we must remind ourselves that our Lord came "not to bring peace, but a sword" *(Mt 10:34)*, to undermine the order of sin and worldliness—remember that other image, that it is the devil who is the prince of this world *(Jn 14:30, etc.)*. We are being incited to misbehave in his court, as well as to behave ourselves in God's court!

The Gospel appeals to our urge to explore, to adventure. It draws us to contemplate enormous vistas which awe and calm the soul, as when God is made to say of himself in the Dialogue of St Catherine, "I am the peaceable sea".[27] But also it draws us into that very different kind of adventure which ends up in dark little backstreets, as when St

Mark, in what is surely one of the most exhilaratingly unexpected comparisons in the whole Gospel, at the very moment of the Transfiguration, compares God with the laundryman: "His clothes were glistening white, with a whiteness no laundryman on earth could achieve" *(Mk 9:3)*.

A very different picture is given us in the Canticle *(2:8, 9)* of the Lord "like a young stag, leaping upon the mountains, bounding over the hills". A similarly rural instinct led the early Church eagerly to take up the story of Orpheus: Christ is the true Orpheus, drawing all nature after him by the beauty of his song.

A picture that can come to our rescue when we feel haunted by the presence of God constantly peering over our shoulder in judgment on all our acts, takes us back to the laundry. This time God is the customer, who has handed over to us the garment of his Holy Spirit, and then left it to us—as in our Lord's own parable of the talents. He will be angry, certainly, if the laundry ruins that garment; judgment is not eliminated; but it is not brooding over us the whole time. After all, a lot can go wrong in the laundry without actually ruining the suit. Not every mistake is irrevocable and fatal.[28]

These are just a few hints. The important thing is that we learn to use our imagination in a way that will lead us into the spaciousness of the Gospel, letting us become the kind of people whose hearts can be enlarged, the kind of people therefore who can keep company with God, whose heart knows no bounds. If we use our imagination in a way which cramps us, the results may look very proper, but we shall end up with a world too small for God. We may find, for instance, that we have opted for a morality that is desperately moral, but devoid of the wild freedom of true Christian morality: a morality that imprisons us in "goodness" instead of freeing us for God. And this is one of the worst kinds of imaginational cramp. We must not think of goodness as something fussy and meticulous, in the manner of the Pharisees. Look rather at the goodness of St Francis, at once shy and colossal; or St Peter, impetuous and foolish, but intensely loyal. Consider the simple, practical goodness of St Thérèse of Lisieux, or the obstinate goodness of St Martin de Porres, or the flamboyantly miraculous goodness of St Vincent Ferrer, or the utterly helpless, broken goodness of St Paul of the Cross.

How unselfconscious true goodness is! Even our Lord did not wish to arrogate it to himself: when someone called him good, he parried it immediately by saying "None is good but God alone" (Lk 18:19). Why should we ever even want to be in a position where we could feel sure of our own goodness?

I cannot resist quoting, to finish up with, from an unknown medieval English writer who translated the famous Scala Claustralium of Guigo II into English, interpolating merrily as he went little gems of his own devising. This is one of his interpolations:[29] "So doth God almighty to his lovers in contemplation as a taverner that hath good wine to sell

doth to good drinkers that will drink well of his wine
and largely spend. Well he knoweth what they be
when he seeth them in the street. Privily he goeth
and whispereth them in the ear and saith to them
that he hath a claret and that all fine for their own
mouth. He taketh them to house and giveth them a
taste. Soon when they have tasted thereof, and they
think the drink good and greatly to their pleasure,
then they drink day and night and the more they
drink, the more they want. Such liking they have of
that drink that of none other wine they think, but
only for to drink their fill and to have of this drink
all their will. And so they spend what they have, and
then they spend or pledge their coat or hood and all
that they may, to drink with liking as long as they
desire. Thus it fareth sometime by God's lovers, that
from the time that they had tasted of the sweetness
of God, such liking they found therein that as drunken
men they did spend what they had and gave themselves to fasting and to keeping vigil and to doing
other penance. And when they had no more to spend,
they laid off their weeds, as apostles, martyrs and
maidens, young of years, did in their time". Scarcely
a puritanical conception of the Christian life! Yet
how firmly and dramatically it leads to the true
austerities involved. In the Canticle *(5:1)*, the bride-
groom invites us, his friends, to "drink deep and get
drunk". That is the context for all our discipline, our
ascetic efforts, our self-sacrifice. God himself, like a
shrewd taverner, has come to us first, to seduce us
from the narrow path of worldly duty, to know the

sweetness of his love. Are we ready to be the prodigal come home, welcomed with a party? Or are we going to insist on being the good boy, the elder brother, prepared only to do his duty, but not to celebrate the feast of love?

Well, for the moment we do not have to decide in any very definitive way; as long as life lasts in this world we can be both brothers in turn. But eventually the question will be put. And which way we answer it, will depend to a very considerable extent on the picture we encourage ourselves to have of ourselves, of human life, of our place in the world.

3 No God but God

God
there is no god but He,
the Living, the Everlasting.

The Koran[30]

Before one of his healing miracles, our Lord asks
"Do you want to be healed?" *(Jn 5:6),* and this
reminds us that our problem is often not just that
we are sick, but that we want to be sick. The Lord
offers to open our eyes, but do we want to see, are
we prepared to accept the responsibility of seeing?

Underneath our mental and spiritual blindness
lurks the far more sinister problem of fallen self-love,
whose roots go deep down into original sin. If we
would accept fully the Lord's offer of grace, I am
afraid that we shall first have to look more deeply
into the obstacles that block his way, obstacles that
are there because we wanted to block his way.

We have already seen some of the significance
of the fact that the Bible presents original sin in
terms of the misappropriation of knowledge; we must
now explore this doctrine further.

Man, so the story runs, was placed in the
paradise of delights, free to do whatever he pleased,
provided he refrained from eating the fruit of the
tree of knowledge *(Gen 2-3),* knowledge "of good

31

and evil", as it says in the Semitic idiom, meaning knowledge of things in general, even, according to one commentator, knowledge of everything, omniscience.[31]

In any case, this knowledge which is, at least for the moment, not conceded to man, is divine knowledge. The tempter entices Eve with this very thing: "God knows that when you eat of it your eyes will be opened and you will be like God, knowing good and evil". And for once he is telling the truth, as God bears out after they have sinned: "Behold the man has become like one of us".

Now this divine knowledge which man usurps is clearly not just information. It is rather one aspect of God's own very being: as St Thomas teaches us, God's understanding is his own substance,[32] that is to say, he *is* his own knowledge. To usurp his knowledge is to make an attempt on his deity. Further, as St Augustine says, "It is not because things are the case that God knows them: they are the case because God knows them".[33] His knowledge is creative knowledge, like that of a creative artist. God knows his creatures in the same kind of way as Charles Dickens knows Mr Pickwick. It is precisely because Dickens knows him so intimately that Mr Pickwick comes alive. So when man helps himself unbidden to the tree of knowledge, it is creative knowledge he seeks to appropriate, he sets himself up as a kind of creator in his own right, trying to be God unto himself.

We can see that this is so in our everyday experience. To say, "Oh yes, I know *him*!" is usually a way of dismissing someone; he is packed up and labelled and stowed away, denied, so far as I am concerned, any further right to change or to grow. Such "knowledge" is not the humble recognition of somebody else existing in his own right; it is an arrogant and tyrannical "knowledge", dictating to others what they are to be.

Or again, self-knowledge can be a very deceptive thing. We can have a picture of ourselves which we take to be the truth, and use it to protect ourselves against all unwelcome challenges and disruptions of our routine. "I know my limitations," we say, "I can't see myself doing that."

When man sets up like this to be his own creator, he is inevitably going to be embarrassed and offended by God's creation, and this is precisely what we find in the Genesis story. The first thing that happens after they have sinned is that Adam and Eve get embarrassed by their own bodies. This obviously includes a reference to the discovery of their sexuality, but we must not mistake the significance of this. Sexuality is not, as has all too often been suggested, just some nasty thing produced by sin. Its most evident characteristic is the degree to which it eludes our rational control, and this makes it a potent challenge to our "omnipotence", to our self-appointed godhead. This is why sanctified sexuality can still be such a great symbol of man's union with God, with the God who is other than man, not just a projection of his own mind. It is also, of course, why unsanctified sexuality causes such a frightful pother!

The essential reason, surely, why Adam and Eve are embarrassed by their own bodies is that their bodies are quite unashamedly created by God, and only to a very limited extent are they subject to their own dominion. Our digestion, for instance, or our breathing get on very well so long as we do not interfere with them. But if you *try* to breathe, you will be likely to do yourself serious damage. Nor can we *try* to walk. We can walk, but most of us cannot *try* to walk, unless we have suffered some serious physical disablement. Our bodies remain an insistent reminder that, whatever we may like to think, we are not our own creators.

So Adam and Eve start disguising themselves, modestly enough at first with a few leaves, but it does not stop there. And when they hear God walking in the garden in the cool of the evening, they go and hide. Now that they have set up as gods unto themselves, living in a world of their own creating, they no longer, in one sense, form part of God's world: he has to ask, "Where are you?" He is on the outside, knocking on our door (cf. *Apoc 3:20*).

A few chapters later on in Genesis we find the same story repeated, only on a larger scale. Men try to build a great tower to storm heaven itself. And just as Adam had to be expelled from Paradise and subjected to decay and death, so now God has to intervene to scatter and divide men, breaking their selfish power, so that there can be at least a pause, a setback, in the awful consolidation of man's tyrannical empire. But man does not give in : beginning with trying to create himself, he cannot help but try to create a whole universe for himself, a universe from which God is systematically excluded, because man is being God unto himself.

If this is what original sin is all about, we can see with horrible clarity why it is that we forget God. Not quite at the root of man, but very close, there is an enterprise which has been going on for millennia, to exclude the remembrance of God, so that we may ourselves be God.

And that is why the great teachers of the spiritual life return so often to the simple scriptural injunction : *vacate et videte,* "be still and know that *I* am God" *(Ps 45:11).* God invites us to take a holiday *(vacate),* to stop being God for a while, and let him be God.

This is one of those areas where we need to use our imagination in the right way. Too often we do not picture prayer in the way that God invites us here; we think of it as a terribly important, serious thing that we have to do, mentally lining it up with all the other important things that pile up on our desks, those weighty matters that depend on us and require our urgent attention. But God is inviting us to take a break, to play truant. We can stop doing all those important things we have to do in our capacity as God, and leave it to him to be God.

If the basic reason why God is crowded out of our lives is simply that we want to be God ourselves,

then it must be so, that the very first point of conversion will be, in however small a way, to stop
being God, and so to leave room for God to be God.

·   ·   ·   ·

A great deal of light is shed on this very fundamental problem of Christian spirituality by a curious
convergence between a piece of ancient theology and
some of the findings of modern psychology.

St Irenaeus, one of the greatest theologians of the
early Church, has a doctrine of the Fall of man
which is rather different from that with which most
of us are familiar and which derives from St
Augustine. St Augustine's view was inevitably
coloured by the particular problems with which he
was faced, and the Church has never accepted it
totally as either exhaustive or definitive. There is no
reason why St Irenaeus should not also be allowed
to have his say.

In his view,[34] the Fall was essentially a matter of
wrong growing up. St Irenaeus believed, as did many
of the early Christians—in marked contrast to the
traditional Jewish belief[35]—that Adam was created
as a young child. The reason why he was forbidden
to eat from the tree of knowledge was simply that he
had to grow up first, and that takes time. Unfortunately, Adam was impatient; in trying to
anticipate his adulthood, by seizing the fruit before
the time was ripe, he thwarted the process of true
maturing. St Irenaeus recognises that one aspect of
this is the disorder that afflicts human sexuality, and

in fact we might say that his presentation of the Fall is, essentially, as a mishandling of the crisis of puberty. The result is that man can now only grow up properly by a painful dismantling of his false grown-upness. To this end, the Son of God "came to be a child with us", so that we could be led back to childhood and then grow up again, this time in a true way, till we come to the full stature of Christ himself (cf. *Eph 4:13*).

Psychological studies confirm that a kind of regression to childhood is sometimes involved even in ordinary mental healing. But even more important, for our purposes, are the studies that have been made of adolescence and puberty. At adolescence a child is confronted with a vast new range of freedom, great new powers which he discovers in himself, great new opportunities in the world around him; but he does not know how to cope with them, precisely because it is all so new, and he has no experience behind him to help him weigh up his situation. In self-defence he is likely to adopt a completely rigid identity for himself. Because he is afraid of the objective freedom that is his, he adopts a stance as if he had already explored it all and discovered all the answers, thereby eliminating unbearable freedom by imposing on himself certain arbitrary options. Ideology thus becomes a substitute for experience, rubrical puritanism (which may be of many different kinds) a substitute for genuine moral growth.

This reminds us of the scriptural picture of sin

as self-creation, entailing, as it does, the rejection or
distortion of our God-given powers for growth and
learning how to live in communion with him and
with one another, substituting tyranny for free relationship (cf. *Gen 3:16*). Instead of entering more
and more deeply into the mystery of God's creativity,
man arrests the whole process with an arrogant "I
know who I am: *that* is who I am". Do we not
know all too bitterly from experience how such an
attitude leads to rigidity and prejudice, an inflex-
ibility that makes any true relationships impossible,
or any creative involvement in the world? The
logical outcome of this can be seen in our mental
hospitals, in the state of complete dissociation from
the real world achieved by some patients. But it is a
road on which we all set out.

And then we move on to build our Babel.
Fascinating research has been done, showing how
modern suburbs embody the same rigid self-
determination of the adolescent, only writ large at
community level. Just how unrelated our picture of
ourselves can be to the real facts of the matter is
shown by the instance of a suburb in an American
city, which was notorious for its very high divorce
rate, about four times the national average, and for
social disorders of every kind. It also had a high rate
of hospitalisation for emotional collapse. Yet when a
respectable black family moved in, the other resi-
dents drove them out on the plea: "We are a community of solid families" (remember their divorce
rate!); "this is a happy, relaxed place, and the

character of the community has to be kept together".[36]

This extreme example shows up how we can build entirely fictitious pictures of ourselves individually and socially, as a defence against a situation that we cannot cope with or contain. The need for such a defence is, of course, an inevitable consequence of our attempt to be God, to be self-creating, self-determining, and to create our own world.

Against this background, certain aspects of Christian teaching take on a new light. It becomes very evident why our Lord tells us to become as little children *(Mt 18:3)*, and what is involved in it; we can see how it is related to the theme of *vacate*, taking a break from being God, to let him be God. Little children do not have piles of important correspondence on their desks, nor rows of shiny telephones to handle all their important business transactions. Becoming as a little child means unlearning the false solemnity of adolescence, unlearning the false maturity and self-importance of ideology and puritanism. It means forgetting to run the world, forgetting to run one another's lives. It means forgetting even to run our own lives.

This sheds light also on St Paul's words that we must not be conformed to this world. If we would learn the true sense in which God is a God of order, we must first unlearn that kind of order which we try to impose on the world and on ourselves and on one another, simply to subject everything to ourselves, to protect us from the wideness and freedom of God's world. The mystics leave us in no doubt that any real growth in prayer, in communion with God, leads us into the desert, into the place of wild wide wastes, where we can get no bearings. We must come out from behind the security of our home-made identity, our self-appointed responsibilities, into the spaciousness of God's world, a spaciousness whose dimensions and orientation we shall only gradually learn to recognise as freedom, within which we shall only gradually discover our true responsibilities.

After all, Egypt under the Pharaohs was an orderly enough place. The Israelites knew exactly where they stood; they knew what they had to do and what resources they had access to. They could count on the fleshpots and cucumbers too, as well as the whips and bricks (cf. *Exod 16:3, Num 11:4f*). But the Lord wanted them out of that security of slavery. And the way to the Promised Land was through the desert, where all they had to eat was manna, *manhu,* which means "What's this?" *(Exod 16:15).* No wonder they sometimes yearned for the good old days of slavery, *anything* rather than this "What's this?" But the book of Deuteronomy tells us plainly what was in the Lord's mind : before the people could be fit to enter the land of his promise, they must learn that man does not only live by nice safe intelligible bread, but "by whatever proceeds from the mouth of God" *(Deut 8:3),* received, in the only way that it can be received, by faith.

This is always the shape of spiritual progress. We

are led out of that kind of order which is built up on sin. That does not necessarily mean a situation of evident outrageous sin, but a situation whose fundamental principle is self-assertion, self-creation, which is therefore sinful at the root, however virtuous its branches may appear.

And one is led out into the desert, into the place of "What's this?", the place where we are fed and tended in a way that eludes our comprehension, precisely so that we may learn to live by faith, by trust in the living God. And so learn not to be God ourselves.

The whole world of our creating must be dismantled, so that all the various bits—all of which were, after all, created by God—can be reclaimed by God and built back into his creation, glorified yet further by the incredible new dignity of the new creation, that new order built up on the union of God and man in Christ. Then we come out from behind the bush where Adam fled in hiding, and God will no longer have to ask "Where are you?" We shall be in his world, visible to him, shining in the light of truth (*in splendore veritatis conspicui*—one of several bold, suggestive phrases in the new liturgy which the translators have, unfortunately, not seen fit to keep.)[37]

For this to happen we must be prepared not just to lose our acknowledged sins, but also, like St Paul, to discard all our own "righteousness" as so much dung, in view of that more wonderful thing which is to know Christ Jesus and to be one with him *(Phil*

3). The Pharisees, as St Paul bears witness, were genuinely good people; but their goodness was home-made. We should always examine the trademark on our goodness, to see whether it is "made in heaven" or only "empire made". We do not want to end up like the Pharisees, whose prayer our Lord described so precisely : "He said this prayer *to himself,* 'I thank you, God . . .'" *(Lk 18:11).*

This does not mean that our attempts to be good and to pray are always inevitably bad. But it does mean that we must be prepared to find that as we grow up further we shall recognise much of our "goodness" and "spirituality" as largely "empire made". And so we must be ready to be dismantled over and over again, until we are entirely remade, receiving our likeness to God from God himself, not trying to seize it for ourselves at the instigation of intruding snakes.

And this means losing that fear which underlay the whole enterprise of self-creation, that fear of the vastness of divine freedom. This does not have to happen all at once. It is possible to loosen very gradually the protective shield of adolescent puritanism, as we gain in confidence and so become more open to the richness, complexity and mysteriousness of God's reality and God's creation.

In fact, we must beware of the danger of "do-it-yourself" conversion. It is possible to dismantle one image, only to set up another. Growing up takes time, as St Irenaeus so insisted. We must not be in too much of a hurry.

But we must allow ourselves, as honestly as we can, to be challenged by the reality of God's world, as it seeps through the cracks in our home-made world, and so gradually learn to trust in him, and so to love him, and so to become docile to his creating and his commanding.

The choice, however obscure it often is in the particular circumstances of life, is very clear in its basic principle : either we surrender to fear, fear of what God has put in us, fear of the world around us that we do not control, fear of God's infinite freedom and sovereignty, and this is inevitably to build up defensive structures of rigid self-determination; or we learn, slowly maybe, to trust and to love. "Do not be afraid, only believe" *(Mk 5:36)*. "Perfect love casts out fear" *(1 Jn 4:18)*. So we must use whatever freedom we have, we must use our minds and our imagination, in ways that will build up love and trust. Also we must let ourselves be honestly hurt by the inevitable inadequacies and frustrations involved in our attempts to be God unto ourselves, so that our motivation to escape from our self-imposed bondage may be strengthened.

But let us make no mistake. This means a real dying to self, a real losing of self. The sentence of death passed on Adam was not just vindictiveness on the part of God, it was a mercy. Nothing would have been more awful than for man, imprisoned within himself, to have eaten of the tree of life, to live for ever. It was mercy that subjected Adam to death, just as it was mercy that frustrated the ambition of

Babel. It is a mercy that is offered to us too : in baptism we died with Christ. Day by day we can live out that liberating death and be born more and more effectively into the real world of God's light and love. There we can keep company with him. The door is open : are we ready to pass through?

4   The Way of Trust

I fled Him, down the nights and down the days;
I fled Him, down the arches of the years;
I fled Him, down the labyrinthine ways
Of my own mind . . .

Fear wist not to evade, as Love wist to pursue.
Francis Thompson[38]

God will know how to draw glory even from our
faults.
Not to be downcast after committing a fault
is one of the marks of true sanctity.
Dom Augustin Guillerand[39]

The Apocalypse gives us some curious hints as to
who it is who will not go into the Kingdom; the list
is headed by "cowards and those without faith"
(21:8). The way out of the whole world-system of
sin, as we have seen, is through faith and trust, and
that means taking a stand against that radical kind
of fear which lurks within the hardness and unyield-

ingness of fallen self-centredness. And there is no doubt that this requires courage; but then, "it is a beautiful adventure to run away to God".

It is not for nothing that we say of someone that "he has the faith", as if that were by itself a sufficient indication of his religious position. Even if we have sometimes used "the faith" in a rather desiccated sense, to mean only that someone knows the right answers to the questions in the catechism, even this points us in the right direction. If we would keep company with God, what is essential and fundamental is that certain things are true, certain things about God and about what God has done. Because these things are true, a certain response and a certain attitude become possible and legitimate for us.

When the writer to the Hebrews says, "A man coming to God must first believe that he is" *(11:6)*, he does not just mean an intellectual conviction of the existence of God. He means a deep acceptance that God is the one who says "I am" *(Exod 3:14)*, whose being and life is foundational and entire. It means, at least in germ, that we give up our pre-occupation with who or what *we* are, with asserting our own "I am", in favour of a more essential and more real "I am" on the part of God. It means that we can now build our home upon the Rock rather than trying, like the snail, to build a home upon our own backs.

If we want to know how we can learn this kind of faith and trust, it is important to recognise at the outset that it is God himself who teaches and inspires faith. It is only by the Holy Spirit that we can call Jesus "Lord" or dare to call God our "Father" *(1 Cor 12:3; Rom 8:15)*. It is God who creates in us the very capacity to receive his own gifts. We must not think of faith, therefore, as something for us to *achieve*; receptivity is itself a gift we must be prepared to receive.

However that does not simply mean the end of all further discussion or endeavour. We can, as they used to say, dispose ourselves for grace; more precisely, we can seek out in ourselves where we are already in a state of receptivity, of letting God be God.

We may make a start very simply with our own bodies. I have already suggested that Adam and Eve, after their fall, became embarrassed by their own bodies largely because they were an insistent reminder that, after all, they had not created themselves, but were creatures of God. And perhaps for most people the easiest way to become conscious of their dependence on God is by way of a simple discovery of their dependence on their own bodily functions. This may not yet be explicitly theological faith, but it is a beginning.

A very simple exercise, practised in some oriental religions, is just to become aware of one's own breathing. It is not a matter of controlling breathing, only of becoming aware of it. This way we find ourselves confronted by one of our most crucial life processes going on very satisfactorily without our deliberate control or supervision. We can begin to discover that there at least we do already know how to receive, we do already trust.

Another very simple exercise is to lie down flat on the floor or on some solid surface, to shut your eyes, and just become aware of your whole bodily situation. Again, you will discover that you are making a real, if primitive, act of faith : you entrust your body to the floor and let the floor hold you up. You find a basis for yourself that is very secure, yet entirely outside yourself. You let the floor in a way support you with *its* "I am". You can take a holiday, relax, enjoy yourself. Then again, what a bustle of activity your body is, and how efficiently it runs itself—all without your permission. You are not God. Here, in a small way, we find ourselves in a world flaunting its "made in heaven" label.

You will also, as likely as not, discover areas of tension in the body; these will be areas that, as it were, do not trust and are determined to hang on to themselves. They are the physical expression of anxiety. And they will not relax simply because you tell them to. But—and this too is a marvellous discovery—if you let them be, and do not interfere with them, accepting them for what they are—and it is important not to confuse acceptance with approval— then you may find that they do relax gradually. Here again we can catch ourselves at it, discover in ourselves the mechanism of trust. And having discovered it here, on however minimal a scale, we shall be able progressively to recognise it elsewhere in our lives.

Now this is not prayer and should not be disguised as a pious exercise. It is just a very humble preliminary. But so often it is precisely because we overlook the humble preliminaries that we get stuck. There could hardly be anything more misleading than the Jerusalem Bible's rendering of *Romans 8:5* : "The spiritual are interested in spiritual things". St Paul was no theosophist! It is not an interest in "spiritual things" that characterises the spiritual man, but a whole approach to life. St Ignatius of Antioch puts it very well : "Even what you do in the flesh is spiritual, because you do everything in Jesus Christ".[40] So we should resist the feeling that we ought to spiritualise everything in some external way; we should not despise the simple bodily things. It is often here that we can learn, or refuse to learn, things of great profit for us.

Our everyday bodily functions can, then, show us how much we already trust, and how peaceful and invigorating a thing it is to have the foundation for our life outside ourselves. And that is an excellent beginning.

But we need to develop also a much more explicit confidence in God, and here again we must use our minds and imaginations. The message of *Psalm 45 (46)* from which *vacate et videte* comes, is clear and emphatic :

> God is our refuge and strength,
> a very present help in trouble :
> therefore we will not fear
> though the earth should change,

though the mountains shake in the heart
of the sea,
though its waters roar and foam. . .
the nations rage, the kingdoms totter . . .
the Lord of hosts is with us,
the God of Jacob is our refuge. (R.S.V.)

It is not only when all is quiet and peaceful that
we can trust in God! St Paul expresses his confidence
in a similar way : "What can separate us from the love
of Christ? Tribulation or oppression or danger or
swords? . . . I am persuaded that neither death nor
life nor angels nor powers nor this present age nor that
which is to come . . . can separate us from the love of
God which is in Christ Jesus" *(Rom 8:35f)*.

A line of meditation arises here in connection with
the resurrection of Christ. The resurrection demon-
strates powerfully that when men have done their
worst, God is still not defeated. Our Lord's death
and resurrection mean that now he fills all things, all
human space *(cf. Eph 4:10)*; he comes to meet us in
the actual sinfulness of our human condition. This is
surely a very consoling thought. The resurrection
encourages us not to be afraid of what anyone can do
to us: "With the Lord on my side, I do not fear :
what can man do to me?" *(Psalm 117 (118):6)*.
Even more reassuring is the thought that we need not
be too afraid even of what we ourselves can do, to
ourselves or to others. Even when *we* have done our
worst, God is not defeated. Often we may be
excruciatingly aware of how we have let other people
down, how we have actively damaged them, hurt

them, made it harder for them to love. Yet God is not defeated. It is not within our power finally to destroy anyone in that utter destruction which is damnation. And even the damage that we do to ourselves by sin need not have the last word. It is always open to us to turn to God in this life and see our sins swallowed up in the ocean of his love. This is, of course, not to say that our sins do not matter; but it is to free us from that crippling kind of anxiety which, more than anything else, prevents us from growing in true charity.

We may go even further. "The anger of men will serve to praise you", it says in *Psalm 75 (76):11*. The events of Good Friday and Easter show us that God actually uses our very hostility, our very rejection of him, to provide the means of our deliverance. He accepts, as it were, our terms and finds a way from where we have placed ourselves through into life eternal.

God's providence does not mean that he has got it all planned out in advance, so that our part is simply to follow. That is a thought that might well drive us to despair : once we had left the right way, who could help us then? We may think of God's providence rather in terms of the way in which he integrates all our free choices, mistakes and sins and all, into his plan. He is that expert dancer who can make dance even out of the stumblings of the most atrocious partner! Our hatred, our fear, become the occasion of our redemption, as we see so clearly on Calvary. And so we need not be so utterly afraid of our own

C

fear and our own hatred. Even though we may not be able to deal with them, God is not defeated.

Another picture that our Lord loves to use is that of the shepherd who goes out to look for the sheep that is lost (Mt 18:12ff). So long as we imagine that it is we who have to look for God, then we must often lose heart. But it is the other way about: he is looking for us. And so we can afford to recognise that very often we are not looking for God; far from it, we are in full flight from him, in high rebellion against him. And he knows that and has taken it into account. He has followed us into our own darkness; there where we thought finally to escape him, we run straight into his arms.

So we do not have to erect a false piety for ourselves, to give us hope of salvation. Our hope is in his determination to save us. And he will not give in!

This should free us from that crippling anxiety which prevents any real growth, giving us room to do whatever we can do, to accept the small but genuine responsibilities that we do have. Our part is not to shoulder the whole burden of our salvation, the initiative and the programme are not in our hands: our part is to consent, to learn how to love him in return whose love came to us so freely while we were quite uninterested in him.

Also we can let ourselves off that desperate question, "Am I in the right place?" "Have I done the right thing?" Of course, we must sometimes acknowledge sins and mistakes and we must try to learn from them; but we should not foster the kind of worry that leads to despair. God's providence means that *wherever* we have got to, *whatever* we have done, that is precisely where the road to heaven begins. However many cues we have missed, however many wrong turnings we have taken, however unnecessarily we may have complicated our journey, the road still beckons, and the Lord still "waits to be gracious" to us *(Isaiah 30:18)*.

If we let these things really speak to us, then we can surely accept our Lord's invitation, indeed his command, to cast all our cares upon him *(1 Pet 5:7)* and let him care for them. We can give space in our hearts for Christ to dwell there, and it is faith that gives him space *(cf. Eph 3:17)*. We can let him dethrone us from being God in our own hearts, and establish there his own rule. We can then let him give us to ourselves, just as at the beginning he gave Adam to Adam. Then we can receive from him all that is ours, all our faculties, all our freedom, our capacity to take initiatives, to make our own decisions, so that our own true independence no longer challenges God's sovereignty but is precisely a most wonderful expression of it, as we receive our freedom day by day, minute by minute, from the creative love of God.

However, just as the simple bodily exercise mentioned earlier involves us in accepting the pains, and the tensions that we may find in our bodies, so also for us to accept ourselves as a gift from God means, for the moment, to accept ourselves as a gift already damaged. And it requires great humility to admit this to ourselves. Receiving ourselves as creatures, as gifts, involves accepting (which does not mean approving) all that goes wrong, and knowing that of ourselves we can do little to set it right; it is he who creates us who also heals and redeems us. In learning how to receive ourselves, we shall learn also how to receive that healing and redemption. The same essential attitude of faith and trust is required.

Once again the kind of mental pictures that we have can greatly help or hinder us. We all tend to be over-impressed by success and measure ourselves against some imagined criterion of success. Maybe we even tend rather to dramatise ourselves as being the hero of our own lives. And of course we all love burrowing around in search of our motives.

But maybe it is really more important just to keep our feet on the ground. In St Thomas' view humility is essentially related to realism about ourselves.[41] We must be humble enough to accept the truth of what we really are, and on the whole that means a muddle of pretty tawdry concerns and ambitions. Most of us are not murderers, not because we are virtuous, but because we are squeamish and cowardly. Most of us would like to act from pure motives, not because we are aware of the demands made by the holiness of God, but because we want the satisfaction of saying to ourselves "well done, good and faithful servant".

We must learn to be what we are, and that means accepting our limitations, our blindness, our confusion about our own motivation, our frequent uncertainty as to whether what we have done was good or bad, helpful or unhelpful; and, accepting all that, to offer it all to God and let him do what he wants with it. Maybe sometimes it is our very vices that can serve him; have we not all of us sometimes been greatly advanced by someone losing their temper with us, or irritating us so much that we just had to learn how to be patient? Maybe that is the service we too are rendering to our neighbours! It is not a very glorious thought. It is God who searches out our hearts, it is God who plans our education. We must be prepared to leave it to him to play his part, trusting even when we do not see, and knowing that, on the one hand, we are not justified simply because we are conscious of no sin, and on the other hand, even if our heart does condemn us, "God is greater than our heart" *(1 Jn 3:20)*.

In *Through the Looking Glass*,[42] when Alice meets the Red Queen and explains that she has lost her way, the Red Queen retorts: "I don't know what you mean by *your* way; all the ways about here belong to *me*." And that is just what we have to learn too: all the ways about here belong to God. We must be prepared to receive ourselves and our way ever anew from God, letting ourselves grow and mature under his care and guidance, prepared to find often enough that we have made mistakes and gone astray, and that even then his love has followed us, integrating our very errors into his plan; at times we shall be loudly and unmistakably convicted of sin by the Holy Spirit. But we shall never ever be in a position to say, "Now I am good, now I am holy". It is for us rather

to hope that we may be like the thief on the cross
(cf. *Lk 23:40*ff) : that, even maybe after a whole life-
time of wandering and stumbling, still at the end we
may be the kind of people who can be saved, whose
hearts can still hear and accept the invitation of God's
love. This does not mean complacency about our
faults; it means looking to the Rock on which we
are built and seeking security only there. He is the
one who says "I am". And his declaration of himself
is the foundation for whatever we may turn out to be.

5 Wrestling at Jabbok

God made a little Gentian—
It tried—to be a Rose—
And failed—and all the Summer laughed—
But just before the Snows

There rose a Purple Creature—
That ravished all the Hill—
And Summer hid her Forehead—
And Mockery—was still—

Emily Dickinson[43]

This way of trusting in God does not mean, as people sometimes fear, an unnatural and inhuman passivity, from which all freedom of initiative and enterprise must be ruthlessly banished. The old image of the doormat in the hands of God was only meant to be a corrective for people whose bristles were particularly stiff; it should not be taken as the sum of all ascetic teaching!

As we receive ourselves from God, seeking to be more and more docile and receptive, we find we are in fact endowed with very considerable autonomy. This is not meant to be exercised against God, certainly; but, rooted within the sovereign freedom of God himself, we are meant to give glory to him precisely by being ourselves free, like him. If sin sets up a false independence, it is no solution to destroy independence altogether. Rather, our freedom must once again be solidly grounded in God's freedom.

If this takes place, we shall discover a very unexpected thing: that there is a kind of obstinacy and recalcitrance which is entirely right and proper, and is even an integral part of humility!

After all, if humility is to do with truth, then it certainly is nothing to do with self-abasement. Accepting the truth of our situation means accepting the whole truth, including the various strengths and talents and abilities that God has given us. It would be preposterous, of course, to act as if any of these things belonged to us by right: but it would be equally preposterous to pretend that they simply were not there!

In fact there is more than one way in which the old enterprise of original sin bears fruit. One way, certainly, is the attempt to dominate everyone and everything. But the opposite determination never to influence or affect anyone or anything is just as much an arbitrary and self-imposed role, and is therefore nothing whatsoever to do with true obedience or humility, but is only another disguised version of original arrogance, just as rigid and unyielding as any other.

The distinguishing mark of true humility is not that it is ready to give in to anyone and anything—that might be merely pathological. It is that humility knows how to be obstinate without being unyielding.

Humility rests simply on the obduracy and recalcitrance of truth itself, and, as Bl. Guigo the
Carthusian says, "We do not defend truth, it defends
us".⁴⁴ There is nothing defensive or anxious about the
obstinacy of humility, it simply *is*, and in simply being
declares itself uncompromising.

Most of our obstinacy covers up a certain degree
of emptiness, a certain degree of dishonesty, of
masquerading and posturing, of being uncertain of
ourselves; that is why it has to be so unyielding. It can
only preserve itself at the expense of a certain ruthless-
ness, maybe even cruelty and disregard of others. All
too often it will be driven to defend itself by deliberate
ideological distancing of itself from others: "I am
this, *not that.*" This is one motivation for sectarianism
and the ghetto mentality. It is not enough just to be
Catholic, or whatever it may be; one feels too insecure
without the further defence of being aggressively "not
Protestant", or whatever the "enemy" may be, until
eventually one's Catholicism will come to consist
chiefly in being as unlike Protestantism as possible.

But true humility is confident enough to be able
not to define itself against anything. Its obduracy is
that of the daisy or the sun, just being themselves;
there is nothing pretentious about such self-assertion,
because it is not particularly self-conscious. It is the
humble man who knows how to stand firm on occasion, and even how to be intransigent, simply because
it never occurs to him to be anything other than what
he is. He has not chosen himself.

And this kind of toughness is in no way contradictory to or exclusive of obedience and yielding. You cannot really shake hands with someone whose hand just goes limp, you cannot embrace someone who just crumbles. It is surely highly significant that the small, symbolic loss of freedom involved in being embraced or having your hand shaken actually cannot take place unless there is also a real element of self-assertion, a firmness of presence.

If we lose our nerve about ourselves and only want to run away and hide, we must accept that as we accept everything else (which does not, I repeat, mean approving of it), as constituting the actual circumstances in which our relationship with God must be worked out. But we should not dignify it with the name of humility; the humility in it will be in our acceptance of the situation, not in our loss of nerve about ourselves.

A person who "has no will of his own" is not a full human being. We are meant to have a will of our own, but that will is meant to be entirely in harmony with the will of God. In our broken-down situation in our sinful world, naturally we shall often find ourselves prey to conflicting wills even within ourselves; our Lord himself experienced this, it seems, in Gethsemane (Mt 26:38ff). But his prayer "Not what I will, but what you will" must not be taken to mean that his own will was laid aside. He *willed* that God's will be done, even at the cost of sacrificing something else that he humanly willed. God does not really want doormats, however useful such an image may be in other ways. He wants our free will engaged in the working out of his will. He therefore requires us to be people who do have a will of our own that we can unite with his.

Humility does not mean having no will of our own; it means accepting—not necessarily approving—our own will as one of the factors in our situation, a factor, therefore, that God may use in the working out of his purposes, for my good or that of others. My will may be misdirected, my determination and insistence may be excessive, and I must recognise that. I shall also run into obstacles caused by the other obstinacies that are around, not least that of God himself, and this will be one of the great means by which my will is educated and purified. Humility means recognising all these things, and not trying to make my will paramount at all costs; it does not mean the simple suppression of my will.

In all of this, the story of Jacob wrestling with God at the ford of Jabbok is tremendously instructive (Gen 32:22-31).

Jacob is travelling with all his considerable wealth after coming to some arrangement with Laban, when he hears that his brother Esau is coming to meet him. Not unreasonably, he fears the worst, and takes steps to placate Esau. "The same night he arose and took his two wives, his two maids, and his eleven children, and crossed the ford of the Jabbok. He took them and sent them across the stream, and likewise everything that he had. And Jacob was left alone. And a man wrestled with him until the breaking of the day. When the man saw that he did not prevail against Jacob, he touched the hollow of his thigh; and Jacob's thigh was put out of joint as he wrestled with him. Then he said, 'Let me go, for the day is breaking'. But Jacob said, 'I will not let you go unless you bless me'. And he said to him, 'What is your name?' And he said, 'Jacob'. Then he said, 'Your name shall no more be called Jacob, but Israel, for you have striven with God and with men and have prevailed'. Then Jacob asked him, 'Tell me, I pray, your name'. But he said, 'Why is it that you ask my name?' And there he blessed him. So Jacob called the name of the place Peniel, saying, 'For I have seen God face to face, and yet my life is preserved'. The sun rose upon him as he passed Peniel, limping because of his thigh." (R.S.V.)

This evocative little tale, one of the literary masterpieces of the Old Testament, shows us what is obviously a major turning point in the life of Jacob, symbolised by the changing of his name to Israel, later usually understood to mean "the man who sees God". And it is at once interesting to notice that it occurs at a time when Jacob is at the height of his fortune. He has pulled off some very successful tricks against Laban, and has come away a very rich man. It is at this moment of triumph that the Lord strikes.

And notice how he strikes. Although Jacob is obviously at a certain disadvantage, terrified as he is by the approach of his brother, caught alone at night, nevertheless Jacob *wins* in his wrestling with God.

I think this mysterious episode from Genesis is one of the best commentaries on St Paul's dictum that "the weakness of God is stronger than men" *(1*

Cor 1:25), the implication of which is clearly that God's weakness is stronger than the strength of men. Perhaps we may take an illustration from judo : God uses the strength of man to bring him into subjection to his plans. God throws us by our own energy, by our own success.

Of course, one aspect of this is that, like Jacob, in our very time of triumph we may be suddenly confronted with the awful precariousness of success, and so find ourselves driven, as he was, to acknowledge our insufficiency before God.

But that by itself would not lead to the radical conversion implicit in the renaming of Jacob as Israel. It is surely the terrifying realisation of what it means that in a very strong sense we have God in our power, that precipitates conversion. The obscure hint given in Genesis becomes too appallingly explicit in the New Testament, with the Son of Man literally given over into the hands of men *(Mt 17:22)*, to do with him whatever they please. And somehow—and this is perhaps the deepest mystery of all—the contemplation of that victory of man over God is what brings countless men, heart-broken, shattered, unmade, humbly seeking forgiveness and new life from the God who made himself known in such weakness. At the end of the book of Job, God convicts Job by a tremendous display of power and greatness; but how infinitely more terrifying and wonderful that he should convict us by a display of weakness.

Yet there it is. That is the truth of God and man. In our arrogance we have appropriated to ourselves

the divine prerogative of knowledge, we have set up as
God in our own world. And we are strong in our own
world. God can and at times does browbeat us; but
for full conversion to be effected, something much
more drastic has to happen. We have to be convicted
of the powerlessness of power, of the futility of being
always on top.

It is the very victory of Jacob which is his undoing.
Perhaps quite unaware of what he was asking, he
demands a blessing. And what could be more expressive of the result than that final picture with which
the story leaves us, of a man limping away in the
light of the rising sun?

Really to meet the weakness, the poverty, the
humility of God, while we are in the full flood of our
strength, our arrogance, our ambition, surely that is
what "disables" us, giving us a new name, leading us
into a light so brilliant that by comparison all our
previous light is seen to be but darkness, and in so
doing making us incapable, at least to some extent,
of simply resuming our career of ambition and the
way of strength (cf. *Lk 16:8*).

This is true humility. Some people seek humility
by dwelling on their own bad points, by comparison
with their good points, by cultivating an awareness of
their weaknesses by comparison with their own
strength. But true humility comes from the juxta-
position of our strength, our self-sufficiency, with the
total and humble reality of God himself. As Isaiah
declared, we shall then find that even our righteousness is not pure in the sight of God *(64:6)*. And our

strength will be seen to be but vulgar cocksureness beside the weakness of Godhead.

So the way to be open to God, receptive and surrendered, is not to try to make ourselves weaker than we are, or to cut down our native obstinacy and self-assertiveness in a merely external way; we should not go after a cultivated, self-conscious humility like that of the man in the old children's book who "prided himself upon having no pride". We must let God wrestle with us, and use our very strength to throw us with. We need not be afraid of the power that is in us; it will meet its match one day in the omnipotent weakness of God.

And then we too shall go away limping into the sunlight. We shall become unfit for a certain kind of success in the world. Jacob had seen God and not died; yet something had died. He could never be quite the same again.

6 The Healing of the Passions: I

Lord, please make all the bad people good,
and then make all the good people nice.

A child's prayer[45]

our attitude towards life
is come easy go easy
we are like human beings
used to be before they became
too civilised to enjoy themselves

Don Marquis *the lesson of the moth*[46]

Conversion and learning to live by faith, by trust in the living God, does not then just mean passivity and discovering our own weakness and helplessness and dependence : it involves also a complete re-orientation of our experience of being strong, of taking initiatives. It makes it possible for us to be receptive even to our own creativity, to be yielding even in being firm and decisive, to be weak even in being strong, poor even in being rich.

And this is what makes possible a deep healing of all our faculties, so that the whole man can be made new in Christ, so that with our whole humanity we can keep company with God.

It is important to be quite clear that it is our

66

whole humanity that is involved in redemption.
There has been a most unfortunate tendency to talk
as if we were basically bad, so that a supernatural
life could only be built on the elimination of the
natural; but this is not what is meant by the "putting off of the old man" *(Col 3:9)*. When the old
monk Alonius said, "If I had not pulled the whole
thing down, I could not have built myself up",[47] he
was not referring to the demolition of his nature, but
to the dismantling of the whole false world of sin,
that false persona that man puts up against what
God creates. And such dismantling makes possible
the recovery of man's true nature, of what man is by
God's creating. Grace first heals our nature, then
elevates it and transfigures it.

If we would become the kind of people who can
keep company with God, we must allow all our
faculties, every aspect of our personalities, to be
healed and converted, so that we will be able to
carry out the divine command to love God with all
our heart and soul and mind and strength *(Mt
22:37; Deut 6:5)*.

And the first thing is to be quite clear that all
our faculties are in themselves good; deep down,
underneath all the disorder of sin, they are good,
springing as they do from the creative goodness of
God himself. Even if it is better to enter into life
blind than to go to Hell with perfect eyesight *(Mt
5:29)*, that does not mean that blinding ourselves
will, of itself, make for our salvation. It would be a
drastic situation indeed that called for such a drastic

remedy, and the Church has never encouraged us to take too literally our Lord's apparent invitation to self-mutilation. If we are to love God with all our heart, we must have all our heart. Even if, in the course of our Christian life, we may sometimes lose the odd finger, or even an eye or two, there is no suggestion that we should try to kill off our hearts. One of the old Egyptian monks said : "If you have a heart, you can be saved".[48] God's promise was that he would take out of us the heart of stone and give us a heart of flesh, a fully human heart, a heart fully alive *(Ezek 36:26)*.

As we grow, then, in the life of faith, trusting in God and so becoming more receptive to the truth of our own nature, we must not be surprised to find our emotional powers developing and maturing. It is not our part to suppress them but in cooperation with God's unfolding grace to see to it that they are progressively more securely rooted in God's creative goodness, and therefore more in harmony with his total purpose.

And this development may take unlikely forms. We must therefore be to some extent prepared in advance, so that we shall be able to make some sense of what happens. This is not just an intellectual luxury, but a very sound precaution for our spiritual well-being.

The basic question is just what our passions, our emotions, are supposed to be, and what their role is meant to be in our lives.

The first point to be made in answer to this

question is that they are meant to be, precisely, emotional and passionate. They are not rational; our reason is a distinct faculty. St Thomas is very explicit that the mind, our rationality, does not have total despotic authority in the human person. Taking a hint from Aristotle, he says that the authority that our mind does have is a kind of constitutional, "political" authority, which must respect the relative autonomy of the other powers that are in us, notably our biological processes and our emotions.[49]

When the mind sets up as tyrant, it is likely to meet the fate of tyrants : assassination. G. K. Chesterton once remarked that insanity is not strictly speaking a matter of losing one's mind, but of keeping one's mind and losing everything else.[50] It is the man who tries to be nothing but mind, whose mind eventually collapses.

Now this is immensely important. Even in the most sanctified and spiritual life, our emotions are still meant to be emotional; they should be harmonised and guided by mind, but not reduced to mere rationality.

Indeed it is one result of original sin, one aspect of fallen man's attempt at empire-building, that we often do try to impose absolute control upon our own emotions. It is part of our desire to create our own identity for ourselves, and to become entirely predictable to ourselves. As has already been suggested, Adam and Eve, after their sin, were affronted by the fact that their own bodily functions were still unashamedly not subject to their pretended divinity.

The same thing happens in regard to our emotions. In psychological terms, we saw how an adolescent, terrified of the new powers he finds within himself, may opt for an absolutely rigid self-determination in desperate self-defence. This is the psychological edge of that deeper tragedy of sin, in which man, wanting to be God unto himself, inevitably has to seek dominion over all God's creation, and so must try to tyrannise over himself as well as other people and things.

It is a great mistake, as well as a complete misunderstanding of ascetic teaching, to suppose that it is always our emotions that are at fault, and that if only they were properly docile to our reason all would be well. We forget that reason is at least as fallen as any other part of us. *All* our faculties are striving after power, and to side with one of them against the rest may sometimes be prudent practical politics, but is never more than that.

The old Platonic image[51] of the charioteer brings out well the relationship between our reason and our emotions. The mind is the charioteer, the passions are the horses. It is not the job of the driver simply to stop the horses, at least not if he wants to get anywhere. However, so long as they are all pulling in different directions, he will not get very far either. His task, then, is to persuade the horses to pull together harmoniously, in more or less the direction that he wants to go. If he succeeds in this, then he can really travel, and travel fast.

In C. S. Lewis' book, *The Great Divorce*, a kind

of myth about purgatory, one of the characters has a mean little lizard on his shoulder, representing sensuality, and it keeps whining to him about all the fun they have had together, even though it is clear that any fun to be got out of the lizard would be pretty thin. And a great angel comes to plead with the man to let him kill the lizard and have done with it. At last the man consents, and the lizard is killed with a great screech, and flung to the ground. And then it begins to grow, and turns into a huge stallion, rearing to go; the man jumps on and gallops away.[52]

In so far as our passions are disordered, they tend to keep knocking each other on the head, so that our emotional life, if it survives at all, is likely to be rather small beer. A man whose passions are ordered and harmonious can have a far more richly and intensely emotional life, fully emotional, but always subject to the over-all guidance of clear thought and vision. He can see where he wants to go, and has the energy to get there.[53]

In C. S. Lewis' story, the author imagines himself watching the lizard beginning to grow, and thinking to himself "it has not worked after all". And it is easy enough for us to get afraid when our emotions really begin to come alive, and get sufficiently disentangled from one another and from the tyranny of reason to make themselves felt. We must rid ourselves of any conception of sanctity that imagines saints to be preposterously demure and dispassionate. We must allow ourselves space for the real human growth that is involved in any true approach to holiness. If we are afraid of the irrational in us, afraid of the emotional, then inevitably sooner or later we are going to have to go back to the routine of original sin, refusing to accept part of what God has created, and trying to set up a new creation, a new identity for ourselves, according to our own specifications.

Of course, in this life perfect equilibrium, if ever achieved, is very very rare. Most of us are likely to be tossed from tyranny of the reason to tyranny of the emotions, and back again. But at least let us be clear that tyranny of the reason is not a whit more holy than its opposite.

St Thomas makes a very significant distinction between what he calls "continence" and what he calls "temperance".[54] Both words now have a rather reduced and specialised meaning; in the older sense, "continence" means holding yourself in, it is the kind of thing that takes place when you would really love to go and knock somebody's head in and manage not to, or when you are on fire with lust and manage not to give in to it. Continence is our emergency brake; it is not a real, fully-fledged virtue such as the saints have, but only a kind of half-virtue which is useful when there is nothing better to hand. The genuine article is "temperance", which means that you simply do not want to go out and assault people, and are simply not interested in fornication. It is not a matter of having disordered desires and managing not to give in to them, but of having ordered desires—and, perhaps we should add, of managing to give in to them. Like Bach's famous clavier, it is a matter of being in tune, an instrument fit for the touch of the divine musician.

·   ·   ·   ·

St Thomas, following the traditional psychology common to both pagan and Christian antiquity, classifies all our emotions under two broad headings, whose most evident representatives are desire and anger,[55] and in fact the Christian ascetic tradition has devoted a great deal of attention to these two emotions in particular. However inadequate this might be if our concern were with scientific psychology, it still provides a useful framework for our present consideration of how it is that we grow in the Christian life, becoming the kind of people who can dwell in the light of God's presence, in the intimacy of his friendship.

Let us begin with anger, bearing in mind that anger is not just a matter of getting cross, even though that may be our most common experience of it; at least as the early Christian thinkers saw it, it is basically our capacity to get worked up about something, leading us to blow up, to smash things, to charge into things.

In *Psalm 4* we read *(4:5)* "Be angry and do not sin". This has sometimes confused people; one translation even says "Be angry but sin not" (R.S.V.), which makes no sense at all. That great Christian master of the spiritual life, Evagrius of Pontus, was right both in his psychology and in his exegesis to interpret the psalm to mean "Get worked up against sin, direct

your anger against temptations and so resist sin".[56]
Anger is given to us, he maintains, for this very purpose. It is that faculty by which we overcome sin and
devils. There is a good illustration of this in the book,
The Exorcist, where the young priest suddenly loses
his temper with the demon, seeing him in all his
ugliness, and that is the beginning of his triumph.[57]
He loses his own life, but he dies with a smile of
victory on his lips.

We have sometimes tended to be too much on
the defensive in our Christianity. There is one ancient
interpretation of our Lord's promise to Peter about the
gates of Hell not prevailing against the Church *(Mt
16:18)*, which takes it to mean—plausibly enough, it
seems to me—not that the Church will stand firm
against the assault of Hell, but that Hell will succumb
to the assault of the Church.[58] It is the Church
storming Hell, just as her Lord did, and not the other
way about. It was in this spirit that the old monks
went out into the desert, the place of demons,[59] or
even settled on high pillars to challenge the demons
of the air *(cf. Eph 2:2)*.[60] Maybe their spiritual
geography was a bit naïve, but their inspiration was
wholly sound.

When difficulties and temptations beset us, we
should charge enthusiastically into battle against them.
Drawing on a more philosophical tradition, St
Thomas treats of the whole emotional area surround-
ing anger as being particularly concerned with tackling
difficulties;[61] it is that part of us which goes *per ardua
ad astra*. It is the source of our sense of adventure;

it is what drives men up mountains and down to the
sea-bed. It is what strengthens us to endure pain and
hardship in what we consider a worthwhile under-
taking.

The Christian virtue of patience is a splendid and
perhaps very typically Christian thing; but it must
not interfere where it does not belong. The New
Testament encourages us to see the Christian life in
terms of a battle *(e.g. Eph 6:12)*. There must be an
element of fighting in it, as well as endurance.

There must also be an element of frustration and
indignation. This world is not as it should be and we
are encouraged to pray: "How long, O Lord, how
long?" *(e.g. Ps 6:4)*. The early Church prayed
urgently for the speedy coming of Christ *(cf. Apoc
22:20)*. It is unfortunate that *Psalm 39 (40):2* should
sometimes be translated "I waited patiently for the
Lord" (R.S.V.); a more accurate rendering would be
"I waited impatiently".

The trouble is, of course, that our anger and our
impatience tend to be misdirected. They tend to be
poisoned at the source by self-pity. Instead of
charging triumphantly through all obstacles into the
full freedom of the children of God, our energy is
too often sabotaged by self-pity, so that it collapses
into mere whining resentment, which then lashes out
indiscriminately, not with a view to clearing a way
through, but simply to win immediate and unthink-
ing satisfaction for our urge to smash things. And
that is not what anger is for.

We are made in the image and likeness of God

and all our faculties, in their true nature, reflect something of God. Anger surely reflects the way in which God's Word is not daunted: it brings light out of darkness, life out of death. Our tragic mistake is to try to *be* God for ourselves, without reflecting him who is truly God. And so we expect our desires to be realised by a mere *fiat,* and then get cross when this does not happen. But just as our desires only have true power, creative power, when they are rooted in God's will and desire, so our anger, our frustration and indignation only carry effective weight when they too are rooted in his determination and omnipotence.

This shows us, then, that it is not enough simply to try to eliminate anger; it must be redirected so that it goes fiercely and enthusiastically against God's enemies, not simply against those who happen to have offended our self-conceit. And God's enemies, we must recall, are spiritual: it is against sin and death and deceit that his war is waged.

It is important to be practical about this whole matter. Anger is there in us and it is meant to be there, only by and large it does not do what it is actually there for. In some people it comes out very freely, but without regard for relevance or proportion; in others it is repressed and goes underground, reinforcing the rigid self-tyranny of our fallenness. In either case it must be freed, integrated and sanctified. And this is likely to be a long and painful process. And if we start from a position where anger is generally repressed, not allowed to come to consciousness to be recognised for what it is, we must be prepared to find that our growth in a life of prayer and trust will be accompanied at first by an apparent increase in bad temper and loss of self-control. The virtue we had built up on self-esteem must be dismantled by the operation of divine grace, and some of the uglier things we had bottled up behind that holy façade are likely to leak out when that begins to happen. For many people the discovery of the true purpose of anger begins with the painful discovery that there is such a thing at all. Those of us who pride ourselves on our patience should prepare ourselves for the worst!

We must indeed know how to use the emergency brake of "continence", but we must not confuse it with true virtue. Ideally it should only be used when necessary, although in fact we shall probably panic sometimes and just grab the brake without thinking. But so far as is possible to us, we should use it only where it is genuinely practical, and where it will at least not block the way to our eventual acquisition of the true virtue of "temperance". Continence always smacks a bit of the nervous, prim self-control that we learned from the serpent.

In some situations, for instance, we may know very well from our experience of ourselves that if we manage not to give vent to some nasty remark, in five minutes time we shall have forgotten all about it and everyone will benefit from our silence. That will be the end of it. That is a reasonable use of continence. But suppose it goes on rankling, suppose we go on brooding; the other person concerned is almost certain to notice that something has soured the relationship and will have to conjecture what it is, and will probably get it wrong, and then he will get upset too ... Maybe a good honest blow-up would have cleared the air. Or again, sometimes if you manage not to lose your temper straight away, you only save it up for a later occasion, when you suddenly explode over something utterly trivial, with a weight of fury quite unrelated to the apparent provocation. And that is hardly just!

There are some situations that, given our actual human and spiritual maturity, we cannot control; our task must be to see that, granted there is going to be an explosion, there be as little dangerous fall-out as possible. And, curiously, blowing up with a bad conscience is actually going to increase fall-out, because we shall then feel the need to justify ourselves to ourselves and maybe to other people too, and so will not be able just to blow up and leave it at that, with a smile and an apology, but will go on interminably explaining everything and showing how we were really in the right. This is, incidentally, something to watch very carefully when we feel tempted to ascribe "righteous indignation" to ourselves. It is almost certainly self-justification.

We must learn a basic kind of simplicity in our behaviour, that allows us just to do whatever we do, and then leave it in the hands of God. He can after all use even our weaknesses and our sins. And it is he who searches our hearts and knows our true motivation. We must very often be content to leave it at that, that he knows us and we do not. Sometimes the Holy Spirit may convict us of sin, and then we must acknowledge it. But often we will not be sure whether we should or should not have blown up, or whether our hanging on to ourselves was prudence or just conceited fear. It is God who is our judge, and that must suffice.

In this way we shall learn what our true resources are; we shall acquire a kind of instinct about when to use the emergency brake. But in the same process our minds will have to learn humility. We shall be less and less able to assure ourselves, from a position of clear vision, that we are doing right. Our eyes must be always towards the Lord *(Ps 24 (25):15)*. It is not for us to want to say prayers of thanksgiving to ourselves, like the Pharisee.

7 Forgiveness

To despair of the patient is to insult the doctor.
Bl. Guigo the Carthusian[62]

One of our greatest difficulties as we try to keep company with God, growing in the kind of intimacy with him that he desires for us, learning to be truly friends with him, sharing his joys and his interests, is that in him such apparently contradictory attitudes are combined. And nowhere is this more evident than in his attitude to sin. In the last chapter we considered how anger is intended to be directed against sin and every kind of evil, and how purified anger is rooted in God's own heart, a mystery expressed terrifyingly and appallingly in the scriptural accounts of how the blessed ones share and rejoice in God's judgment of his enemies (cf. *1 Cor 6:2; Ps 67 (68):24*). Yet it is precisely here that we come up against the even more inscrutable mystery of God's forgiveness.

That this is crucial for our life of prayer is indicated by our Lord himself. His one and only comment on the prayer which he gave to his Church is that if we do not forgive, we shall not be forgiven *(Mt 6:14f)*. That seems to be the test case of whether we are capable of walking with God in the kind of relationship that prayer involves.

The ascetic writers warn us that this is no light matter.[63] It is easy enough perhaps for those with little sense of the enormity of sin to practise forgiveness. But as our vision clears, the temptation to rigorism and abuse of anger grows apace. This is, perhaps, the especial occupational hazard of spiritual people, who are, I fear, notoriously intolerant. (Though, incidentally, it is some consolation for us to find that even apostles were a prey to this: Paul and Barnabas had to separate, so great was the dissension between them *(Acts 15:39)*, yet God used each of them for his work of reconciliation. "The anger of men shall serve to praise you".)

Our problem is how to grow both in clarity of vision and in compassionate tenderness of heart. It is with that that we must concern ourselves in this chapter.

The first point to notice is that forgiveness is not the same thing as indifference. Forgiveness includes judgment, the judgment that something is a sin. It is easy enough for us to go to confession week after week confessing our polite little misdemeanours and accepting forgiveness for them, because we ourselves do not take them very seriously as sins. But it is a very different matter when we manage to do something that does actually shock us, whether it be because our conscience has become more sensitive or just that our behaviour has become worse. Then we discover how ugly sin is, and how real. Sin does actually hurt people. It is not just an affair of a minor inconvenience or two, but actually ruining someone's life, breaking their heart, making it impossible for them to trust, doing them out of their job or their reputation... Sin is foul, it is offensive, it is the most offensive thing in the universe.

And it is precisely sin that is forgiven. Real sin, sin that stinks.

The Apocalypse warns us not to be cowards, if we want to get into the kingdom of God, and there is a particular kind of cowardice called squeamishness. It is no good being squeamish about sin. Forgiveness is not something for people with weak stomachs. Take a good look at the cross of Jesus Christ if you want to know what sin is, if you want to know the raw material of forgiveness. It is not a comfortable sight.

Our Lord warns us to count the cost before we start building towers *(Lk 14:28ff)*. It is all very cosy at the beginning, with garden parties and the Lord Mayor laying the foundation stone. Every convert, every novice knows how lovely it is to be a Christian, and what fun it is to be holy. But after the tea comes the hard work, the dirty work. Living with God means living in the light, and the light shows things up. The coming of the light into the world cannot help but be judgment *(Jn 3:19)*, because it confronts us with a straightforward choice: either to let the light show things up, or to bury our heads and pretend that nothing has happened.

Living in the light of God involves a readiness

to see some ugly things, and many of them will be in our own hearts. We must be prepared to discover just how deep the wound of sin is in our humanity. Some ancient ascetic writers recommended a practice whose most famous recent exponent is Chesterton's Father Brown:[64] entering imaginatively into the heart of every kind of criminal, knowing that that criminal is oneself; finding the murderer, the blackmailer, the thief in oneself.

This must not be confused with attempts to work up a false humility, by ascribing to oneself wickedness of which one is, actually, incapable. False compunction is worse than useless, as St Dominic knew well, when he told his young men to weep for sins, and added that if they had none of their own to weep for, there were plenty of other people's sins.[65] Forced contrition is only another modification of that basic stance of original sin, in which we try to create ourselves according to whatever specifications we may happen to want at the moment.

It is not an artificial sense of our own sinfulness that is required, but the gradual painful perception of what there really is in our own hearts. Please God, much of it may never reach as far as action. But our Lord tells us *(Mt 5:22)* that even so slight a thing as saying "Fool!" to our brother puts us in the same boat as the murderer. Some people's temper has more obstacles in its way and so does not get as far as actual murder, but the root is the same.

Learning to live with the God who forgives means learning not to be squeamish about the real nature

D

of sin. Forgiveness is nothing whatsoever to do with connivance or indifference. It is as robust as sin; indeed, more robust.

The robustness of forgiveness is seen in the story of Jesus. The strength of sin is displayed in all its crudity on Calvary. But life wrestled with death, and by dying defeated death. This is the confidence that makes it possible for us to look sin squarely in the face. Sin does not have the last word. God takes the deadest of dead ends and makes it into his highway.

And this brings us to the next point. As we become more aware of sin and more aware of its sheer ugliness, there is a danger that we will become too preoccupied with ourselves and our sins and our need of forgiveness, cleansing and healing; and then we may actually miss the point of forgiveness.

Our Lord gives us a severe warning in his parable of the servant who owed his master an incredibly large sum of money and was let off *(Mt 18:23ff)*. The fact that we refer to it as the parable of the unforgiving servant already lays us open to the danger of misunderstanding it. Our Lord presents it, not as a story about servants, but as a story about their master. It was because he was too concerned with himself that the first servant, having been let off his enormous debt, went straight out to demand payment from one of his fellow servants. We are not told what was going on in his mind, but it is easy to guess. Presumably he had been worried to distraction by his colossal debt, and came into his master's presence thinking only of that, only of his own prospects. When he heard that all was remitted, he did not give a thought to his master's generosity, but only to the fact that his problem had vanished. So he went away still thinking only of himself; and, feeling shaky and in need of reassurance, he went off, as we so often do, to take it out on somebody else, to restore his self-esteem by the exercise of power. He had missed the essential point of what had happened to him.

In one of his arguments with the Jews in St John's gospel *(8:24)*, our Lord says to them : "If you do not believe that I am, you will die in your sins". This invites us to go much deeper into the nature of forgiveness. Our sins are taken away because we believe that he is, that Jesus is the full declaration of God's "I am", present in our midst; and our faith is, as we saw, essentially the acceptance of this fundamental truth of God's being, essentially that attitude in us which allows room for him to be God.

Forgiveness, then, is something to do with the penetration of the totality of God's life into our fallen world ("in him it pleased all fullness to dwell") *(Col 1:19)*. And in the face of such totality, such purity, such entirety of life, sin cannot stand. Death is swallowed up in life, sin is swallowed up in divine perfection.

This is why we are invited to *celebrate* the sacrament of penance, which we could hardly do if its primary focus were upon our sins. The centre of forgiveness is God himself. "Forgiveness of sins" is, in fact, one designation of the Holy Spirit.[66]

Forgiveness, then, is very much more than just a way of wiping clean a slate so that we can revert to the *status quo ante*. It is very much more than just the timely solution to our problem. It is the incursion of God himself into our world. And this incursion is always both judgment and deliverance. The Holy Spirit, who is remission of sins, is also the one who convicts the world of sin.

Perhaps we can glimpse something of the way in which God's wrath and his forgiveness are related. If anger is that faculty of fury which breaks through difficulties and smashes obstacles, then surely our sin—because God in his mercy accepts it to be so—is the obstacle of obstacles in the way of the full revealing of God's glory in creation. God, in his love for us, has determined that, in some profound way, our glory is to be involved in his and his in ours, so that redemption is, in a mysterious way, almost necessary to him. His anger means that he "will not give his glory to another" *(Is 42:8)*. He will not compromise, he will not surrender. He sends his Word to confront our sin, his Word which penetrates so deeply and subtly that it divides even soul from spirit *(Heb 4:12)*, and he sends it precisely to effect a great judgment, a *krisis*, to use the Greek word, which means literally "separation". He wills to separate us from our sins, even though they have become intimately part of us. Forgiveness is one aspect of this unyielding judgment of God, which is backed by the whole flood tide of his determination.

If we would learn what forgiveness means, then, we must be tough, we must be ruthlessly realistic, with the realism of God himself, recognising both the magnitude of the problem, the horror and deep-seatedness of sin, and the grandeur of the solution, neither reducing sin to mere moral error, nor forgiveness to a kind of business transaction. In the one there is a whole abyss of foulness, in the other a seething furnace of perfection, which we may call love, provided that we know what fury, what terror that word contains (cf. *Cant 8:6f*). "I am God the jealous."[67]

.   .   .   .

Once we see that God himself, in his own vital perfection, is at the centre of forgiveness, then it becomes clearer why our Lord is so insistent that being forgiven is inseparable from forgiving. We cannot let the truth of God's being penetrate our own sin, so that we may be forgiven, if at the same time we are trying to exclude one essential aspect of that truth.

In a sense, it should not matter too much whose the sin is that is being forgiven. It is not the actual specificity of the sin that is interesting, but the marvel of a life that can live through death, the wonder of a holiness that can "be made sin" for us, to vindicate holiness (*2 Cor 5:21*).

As we walk with God in growing love and intimacy, learning his ways, beginning to be sympathetic to his thoughts and attitudes, we must be prepared to learn to see sin from his point of view. We must be prepared to see sin, our own sin and that of others, from the vantage point of the Cross.

And that involves a complexity of identification that is quite amazing. On the Cross, Christ, who is God and man, made himself sin for us, becoming a curse, so that he might be identified fully with all sinners. In being united with him, we are united with ourselves in a new way; we are also united with all other sinners, so that, as I have said, we must not be too preoccupied with whether it is *my* sin or yours. But also on that same Cross, our Lord identified himself with every victim of every sin. And so in being united with him we are also united with the victims of sin, including—and what a mystery of reconciliation is lurking here!—including the victims of our own sins. We are also united with the victims of every other sin, and this is one of the main sources of true intercession and vicarious suffering.

From this vantage point we can begin to learn how to recognise to the full the intense horror of sin, while at the same time viewing all men with compassion and a sense of belonging.

It is all too easy for us to be censorious of others, as if we and they were of different species. If we really learn to recognise the roots of sin in our own heart, as recommended by Father Brown, then, as St Bernard teaches us,[68] we cannot help but learn compassion. We shall discover that we are all in the same boat.

Then our forgiveness of one another will not be

supercilious, any more than it will shrink to mere conniving; it will spring from a true sense of identification.

And, going with this, we shall learn to rejoice in the whole of God's work of forgiveness. The essential joy of forgiveness will be the same, whether it is I who am forgiven, or someone else—even if that someone else has sinned against me. As a sinner, he and I are in the same boat, and it is relatively unimportant that I happen to be the person he has hurt. The crucifixion of Christ shows us how far we must be prepared to go with this. Being hurt means being hurt, and yet still we may feel compassion for and identification with the one who hurts us. He hurts me, but I too am a murderer. And as receivers of God's grace, again we are in the same boat. It is far more wonderful and worthy of my attention that God should be present in that sinful situation with the full majesty and joy of himself, than the paltry fact that it is I who was sinned against.

Perhaps the most mysterious aspect of all, though, is that we must learn to forgive those who have sinned against others, not us. It is easy for us to take up the very moral-looking position, "I do not mind what he does to me, but I can never forgive what he did to the children". And we may feel that we have no right to forgive sins committed against others; quite properly we shall wish to avoid the kind of selfishness which does not mind what happens, so long as I do not get hurt.

But yet, the forgiveness of God knows no limits.

If we are to walk with him, we must not set limits where he sets none. We cannot keep joyful company with him, if our hearts are hardened against those whom he forgives. It is our great privilege to be involved in his enterprise of forgiveness; as we have seen, our Lord treats this as an essential indication of our fitness to pray.

Being united, in Christ on the Cross, with all the victims of every sin, we do have the right to forgive; a right not to be exercised in trivial indifference, but in the agony of involvement. Actually, there is a great ministry here which we can perform for one another. Often it is morally impossible for me to forgive someone who has harmed me; I may want to forgive, but somehow find it beyond my powers. The support of my brothers and sisters in Christ, forgiving for me, may well be the means by which eventually I too can learn to forgive.

Quite apart from that, it is essential, if we would truly pray, that we leave judgment to the Lord, and do not harden our hearts in an unforgiving spirit, whatever has been done by whoever to whomever. That is the measure of love which is required of us; maybe we shall not achieve it all at once, but we are required at least to grow, and not to refuse growth when it is offered, so that at the end we may be found perfect as our heavenly Father is perfect.

It does not really matter so very much who has done what, or to whom he has done it; we are all in the same boat, for there is not one who has not sinned *(Rom 3:9ff; Gal 3:22)*. But in the midst of this whole world of sin, stands he whom we did not know, whom we had shut out by sin, the very Word of God, containing in himself all life, all sweetness, all perfection. And into that abyss, that ocean of love, all sin can be tipped, evacuated, annihilated. In face of such great doings, we should not be paltry-hearted. Let our hearts expand, to comprehend with all the saints just how wide and deep and high is the heart of God. There justice, with all its requirements, embraces peace. And surely here is the place of prayer.

8 The Healing of the Passions: II

i was talking to a moth
the other evening
he was trying to break into
an electric light bulb
and fry himself on the wires

"it is better to be happy
for a moment
and be burned up with beauty
than to live for a long time . . ."

i do not agree with him
but at the same time i wish
there was something i wanted
as badly as he wanted to fry himself

Don Marquis[69]

We must now turn our attention to that other great area of our emotions which centres on our desires, our appetites.

Once again our task is not one of suppression, but of healing and wholeness. Man was created with appetites, he was meant to want things. He needs air and water and food, affection and joy; and since man does not just operate under the compulsion of blind instincts or gravitational forces, he experiences his needs as conscious desire. All this is quite natural, it is part of what man is as a creature of God.

But all his other appetites are rooted in one most basic need, and that is his need for God. All creatures, in whatever way is appropriate to them, have some kind of gravitational tendency towards God.[70] Man, in accordance with his nature, contains this tendency in a peculiar form, which must be realised freely and consciously as love, but it is at least as deeply rooted in his instincts as human love is rooted in his sexuality.

In fact, according to Christian tradition, which is in this matter considerably more radical than Freud himself, just as there is a deep interconnexion between all our desires and our sexuality, so sexuality itself is a manifestation of an even more fundamental urge. St Paul hints at this when he suggests that marriage itself is symbolic of a more basic union, that between God and man *(Eph 5:32)*. Sexuality itself is, as it were, one specification of a more profound instinct, which is man's innate and ineradicable need for God.

It is important to make this point, because we can easily be terrified of our own sexuality. It obviously appears as one of the most disordered and unmanageable aspects of being human in this fallen world, and so down the ages people have always been tempted to treat it as a thoroughly bad job, which we should have nothing to do with at all.

But self-castration in any form is something the Church has not accepted. All our faculties are rooted in God's creative act and are therefore essentially good, however warped and wounded they may have become. Our task is to learn what they are really for, so that they may be drawn back into harmony.

In fact we must go even further. Man is God's image in the temple of this world, and we must venture to say that man's desires are, in some extraordinary way, the image of God's desire. Dionysius the Areopagite intimates that there is, in the last analysis, only one love, the love that wells up eternally within the Godhead.[71] All created appetite is only a partial expression of and sharing in that divine love. Our desires can only be understood in the light of God's desire—and the revelation of God in Jesus Christ legitimates such language once and for all. There is an essential harmony between God's desiring and man's so that it is possible for God and man to be united within a single person in Jesus Christ. That union is the type of our union with God, and the index of what true human desiring is.

Man *with* all his funny little wants is to express the likeness of God; under the guidance of God himself, we must relearn how to have desires that are not disordered and contradictory, but a true expression of that love which is the life of God. And so, however much we may have to use the emergency brake of "continence", we must never make it an end in itself.

And we must be aware that there is something very frightening for fallen man in his desires. Desire is always a reminder to us that we are not self-sufficient.

Even if it is only an ice-cream that you want, it punctures your world, threatening the whole enterprise of original sin. It is therefore very much in the interest of our vanity to try to eliminate or at least inoculate desires.

One of the commonest ways we do this is by attempting to cut our desires down to a size that we can safely manage. Instead of letting ourselves be drawn out of ourselves by our desires, by the things that attract us, and so losing our conceited self-control, we prefer to identify very precisely that what I "really" want is something that is entirely within my grasp. It would be interesting to study carefully the way we use that word "really" in such a context! Men who love God are told that what they "really" want, but cannot admit, is sex (generally in a quite dehumanised, impersonal, way, it seems). Such reductionism crops up all over the place, and it is an integral part of the propaganda of original sin. *All* we need to make us happy is—whatever they happen to want to sell us at the moment. Advertising goes back to the snake in Eden!

One common form of this is that kind of idolatry which tends to occur when people fall in love. Then you identify some other human being as the source of all your bliss, and try to possess him or her. When the relationship then begins to show the inevitable signs of strain, instead of recognising that the initial demand and expectation was unreasonable in the first place, people just conclude that it was the wrong girl, the wrong boy.

We can do the same thing with a job, a religious order, a friendship. We want the "ideal" job, the perfect religious community, the friend who can be an *alter ego* with nothing missing.

And then of course we get frustrated. Then we have a choice: we may try to deceive ourselves with false grown-upness, assuring ourselves that we have "really" got what we "really" wanted and must make the best of it, declaring ourselves content by an autocratic edict.

Or we can simply opt for cynicism, and harden our hearts never to love again, never to want anything, never to make ourselves vulnerable like that again, because it is all too painful.

But the result of that is death. Christians are not to be cowards, we must not be afraid of pain. We must not shut our hearts against desire, but learn how to desire rightly, so that our whole wanting apparatus can be healed, so that eventually it will find its full satisfaction in him who alone can satisfy us.

We cannot learn to love God by learning not to love. If we kill off in ourselves the faculty we have for desire, then we shall paralyse our faculty for loving God. This is perhaps a particularly urgent temptation for those who profess chastity, or who have had unbearably painful experience of trying to love. Chastity can be confused with rock-like indifference; but rocks cannot love God. They may be very chaste, but only in a way which precludes the very purpose of being chaste.

True detachment from creatures comes not from rock-like indifference, but from the strength of our central orientation towards God, which frees us therefore for realistic relationships with creatures. If we are looking for our basic satisfaction from God, then our other appetites lose their bitterness. We can enter into full and rewarding relationships with other people without making impossible demands, without expecting more from them than they can actually give. Because we are letting God be God, we do not expect anyone or anything else to be God.

Medieval spiritual writers had a very full doctrine of charity in this connexion. They teach us that we must learn how to rest in God, trusting in him and being patient with ourselves, so that our hearts are open for the sowing of his divine seed, the seed of true virtue. Gradually we shall as a result be permeated by the influence of the Holy Spirit, until he takes possession of our whole heart. This they refer to as the gift of the Holy Spirit, and its name is charity. And the result is the total transformation of all our appetites and interests, so that quite spontaneously we shall think and feel in accordance with God. Even our most trivial thoughts and desires will express his love which dwells in us and has become the source of our loving.[72] We can recognise in this also a description of fully-fledged "temperance", in which we do not have to keep hanging on to unruly aspirations and yearnings, because our hearts are at peace and in order.

The practical question now arises: how do we

get there? How do we learn to desire rightly, what are the signposts on the way?

First let me repeat that we do not learn to desire rightly by trying not to desire at all. The parable of the prodigal son brings this out well. It is one of the stories that our Lord told about two brothers, the essential point being that one of them appears to be good ard is not, while the apparent scoundrel is the one who turns out all right. The simplest form of it is the story of the two brothers told by their father to go and work in the fields *(Mt 21:28ff)* : one says "No" but then goes and does it; the other says, "Yes, of course, father; anything you say", and then does not go and do it.

The story of the prodigal son is more elaborate *(Lk 15:11 ff)*. Again there is the good brother, the one who stays at home, and this time he actually does do all that he is told to do. And there is the younger brother, the hero of the story, who gets a bit restless and wants to leave home. So he asks for his share of the inheritance and goes off to enjoy himself. And enjoy himself he does, by all accounts; only it is a rather fruitless enjoyment, leaving him eventually bankrupt. And, since innerspace and outerspace often do seem to reflect each other, there is a famine too. So he is hungry. And this makes him think; and as a result of his thinking, he concludes that he might just as well go back home. So off he sets, ready with a nice little speech, humble to the point of being abject, begging his father to take him on as a labourer.

And we know what happened next. His father saw

him coming and rushed out to meet him and gave
him a great big hug and ordered a party. And the
poor boy had to forget all about his humility. He
had to be humble enough to swallow his humility and
be the hero of the day. Meantime, his worthy brother
went off in a huff.

The elder brother is a character study in
Pharisaism, in that kind of goodness which, if you
insist on it, can only lead to damnation. He is scrupu-
lous, honest, hard-working, does what he is told,
and is entirely satisfied with life—or likes to think
he is; his behaviour at the end of the story casts
some doubt on it. But he is quite unaware of the
wealth of love which was there, just waiting for him
to draw on it. It had never crossed his mind to ask
for a party! His world was entirely tamed and colonised by himself, it was pure "Egypt": he knew his
job and his rations, did the one and ate the other,
and that was it. He never learned to appreciate his
father's generosity, and so at the critical moment he
found himself condemned, by himself, to remain outside, sulkily content with the thought of his own
righteousness.

The younger brother is very different. From the
very beginning he wants something. He is restless. At
first, like most of us, he thinks that what he wants is
money and all that money can buy. And having got
his money he sets off to live riotously. But then he
discovers that such enjoyments—real as they are—
are not enough. He discovers the bankruptcy of certain kinds of satisfaction. And this forces him to

discover a much more fundamental need. The experience of famine cuts down and purifies his appetites :
it is no longer the life of luxury that he wants, but
just something to eat. He has discovered his dependence, and the incompleteness of his world in itself.
And his first reaction is to cringe and creep.

And in his abjectness he could, in his own way,
have become just as uptight as his good brother. There
is a Pharisaism of the publican. C. S. Lewis warns
us of the danger of the "all I want" syndrome,[73]
insisting ruthlessly on our own requirements, veiling
our self-centredness with the apparent modesty of
our demands. The prodigal come home could have
insisted on not being worthy of a party, nor even of
being a son. But he did not. Perhaps because his
need was so immense and so fundamental, he was
prepared to receive far more than he had asked for.
Having learned one true desire, he could accept the
unlimited generosity of his father.

The role of desire in his story is evident throughout. He knew and accepted that there was something
he wanted, even if at first he looked in all the wrong
places for satisfaction. And this made it possible for
him eventually and after long wandering to receive
and accept a quite gratuitous and unexpected flood
of love from his father; and we may presume that he
came to see that that was, after all, what he had
really wanted the whole time.

C. S. Lewis' two autobiographies[74] are structured
on this same point. He was, he tells us, surprised by
joy, and had to devote his life thereafter to trying to

identify the source of that joy, examining various obvious candidates, such as sensuality, only to discover at the end that it was God himself wooing him through the experience of joy.

St John of the Cross tells of a similar process, which he calls "questioning the creatures".[75] Something wounds you, something gets into you, that dislodges you from complacency, from being God to yourself. You discover an ache, a hole in your heart, a need. So off you set to look for "him whom my soul loves". And you meet creatures first. And they say to you, "What you are looking for is not here, but he has passed by, scattering beauty as he went". What attracts us in creatures is something of *his* beauty. The creatures are honest : they tell us plainly that they are not enough to fill that hole in our hearts. We must be honest too, honest enough to hear them. Often we may not be as efficient as St John of the Cross at getting through this stage. We may dally for a long time with creatures, trying to persuade ourselves that this is what we "really" wanted. But it is not the creatures that deceive us. They testify plainly by their very beauty that someone else has passed by.

So our experience of being attracted, of feeling desire, is tremendously important; and so also is our experience of frustration. Frustration should not lead us to harden our hearts, and make ourselves insensitive and invulnerable, but should remind us that we are being referred on, directed further.

Of course sometimes we do need to use the

emergency brake, we do need just to hang on, to prevent ourselves giving in to some desire. But we should use it sensibly as a practical expedient, not making us more and more stolid and rock-like, but laying us more and more open to that perfection of love which will transform and integrate all our wanting. Restraining ourselves from immediate gratification of every whim should lead to a real education of our desires and tastes.

And this means learning how our love proceeds from and is situated within God's love. Then our joy in creatures will be a part of his joy in his own creation, a part of our joy in him.

Let us think of Adam again and imagine what is involved in his being called to name the beasts (Gen 2:19ff). Surely this was not to be just an exercise in domination, Adam simply imposing names, irrelevantly and superficially, on God's creatures. Surely it was more a matter of Adam entering sympathetically into God's creativity, and so entering at the same time into a kind of intuitive union with the animals themselves; so he would discover their names in discovering their identity as it sprang from the creative love of God. Adam naming the beasts was a manifestation of God's love for them. Imagine Adam faced with the first kitten. Entering into God's own incredible joy and love and humour, he would hear, as it were, a kind of whisper in the very heart of God, a whisper echoed in that little ball of fluff. And Adam, in trembling and amazement, would utter the mystical word "kitten".

In our relationships with one another it is God's loving that is fundamental. It is with his love that I am to love my friend, making his love my own, as it were, so that it is truly my love, truly a human affection, a human emotion, with all the passion and wonder that that involves. The human heart of Jesus is the perfect expression of the divine love of God, and it must be the model for our loving.

That is why sometimes it may even be right for my friend to think that I am God. True affection carries this awesome responsibility. Sometimes it may be that the nearest someone can get to loving God and trusting him is in letting me love him and so trusting me. I must pass on his love and trust to God, who is the source of what is true in my love.

Even the love with which I love myself is involved in this: it too must be plunged back into the creative love of God which is the very source of my existence and my identity.

All true loving begins with God, and that is why it is such a terrifying thing. Just as the adolescent, confronted with the fearsome powers revealed by puberty, will tend to put up a defensive barrier, so we will all of us tend to panic when confronted with the even more immense and unmanageable power of charity. Flowing as it does from God himself, with the burden of his eternity and infinity behind it, how could we ever dream of trying to control or manage it? We may sink in it, we may swim in it; but we shall never be able to put it in a bottle and store it away safely in the refrigerator.

Our part in that loving is implanted in us in the first place by the very act of our creation. It is renewed and enhanced by the indwelling of the Holy Spirit given to us at baptism. And so at no stage is it simply something we can decide about. In a very true sense we cannot decide to love God, any more than we can decide to breathe or to be alive. In a reduced sense, we can decide to love God, in that we can decide to stop stopping ourselves from loving God, just as we can hold our breath and then stop holding it. But essentially it is something going on under God's control, and it is something as natural to us as any of our natural functions. We must not *try* to love God; we must become the kind of people who will discover that we *do* love God, and then accept it and let it come to its full flowering.

And then our hearts will be progressively conformed both to their own true nature and to the will of God. It is very important not to have a wrong picture of the relationship between God's will and mine. God does not want them to remain apart, in such a way that we shall be always "sacrificing our own will" against our will in favour of his. He wants us to *want* what he wants.

That is why we do well to be suspicious of flamboyant martyrs, people who always go around with an air of self-sacrifice. Of course, often our truest desire to do God's will may be in conflict with other natural and legitimate desires, and this is exemplified in our Lord's agony in Gethsemane; there may be a real crucifixion. But even so, at the end of it, we shall not, if we are truly motivated by charity, be able to say with some self-satisfaction, "Now I have really done something for God!" We shall still have to say that we have only done what we really wanted to do. And that gives little ground for vanity. Our Lord himself said how he longed for that Passover meal in which he would consecrate himself for sacrifice *(Lk 22:15)*; and St Catherine[76] explains that it was even a kind of relief to him when his terrible ordeal began, so hungry was he to give himself to the uttermost for love of us.

Christian growth should make it harder and harder for us to identify God's will as something external to us, so we shall be less and less able to indulge in the pleasant feeling of a pampered good conscience.

God is not just the policeman trying to keep us in order, or the examiner waiting to see our papers; he is also the great seducer, wooing us into his paradise of delights, so that his own joy may be in us, and our joy may be full. And this is that full human freedom, which Peraldus sums up as being the condition of a man "whose heart is large from the abundance of grace, so that he does whatever he does for God, simply because he wants to" *(mere voluntarie)*.[77]

9 Growth in Freedom

*I must endure the presence of two or
three caterpillars if I wish to become
acquainted with the butterflies.*

Saint-Exupéry[8]

"Love and do what you like."[79] This well-known
text from St Augustine sums up in a nutshell the
Christian doctrine of freedom and obedience. As we
saw in the last chapter, as charity becomes more
and more operative in our hearts, our spontaneity is
transformed at the root so that all our thinking and
feeling and wanting is anchored in God's will. And
this leads to the apparent paradox that we must
become both more free and more obedient. In the
medieval theory, the gift of charity functions through
the gifts of the Holy Spirit which make us docile to
the particular inspirations of the Holy Spirit, so that
our lives are no longer just run by our human vision
and prudence, but by the vision and prudence of
God himself. But at the same time—and this is
pointed out emphatically by John of St Thomas in
his treatise on the gifts of the Holy Spirit[80]—
"where the Spirit of the Lord is, there is freedom"
(2 Cor 3:17). This docility to the Holy Spirit does
not constrain us, it sets us free. In the words of the

106

old prayer, "To be his slave is to reign like a king",[81] or as the Book of Common Prayer put it, "whose service is perfect freedom". Living by the gifts of the Holy Spirit, which are, so to speak, the limbs of divine love, must not be thought of as an exterior conforming of our deeds to some blueprint or set of instructions given to us from on high. It is rather a growth in instinctive sensitivity to the will of God; rather than an anxious attitude of trying to "get it right", it will be a strong and sound confidence that our inventiveness, our freedom, will suggest to us things that are pleasing to our divine friend and lover.

There is always a tremendous risk involved in giving anyone a present. We may try to minimise it by asking the person concerned what exactly we are to give him; but how much more precious and fruitful it is for loving relationship, when we are able to choose something, quite independently of any suggestion, that will make our friend exclaim, "Why, that's just what I wanted!"--a want, maybe, which he only discovered in the very receipt of our gift.

That is perhaps a sounder model—though of course only a model—of our relationship with God in the Holy Spirit, than some other pictures of obedience that have been used.

According to St Thomas it is an essential privilege of our humanity that we are the source of our own actions.[82] We are not just moved around like puppets, we move ourselves: we are free. The Holy

Spirit, claiming us and our activities for God, does not annihilate that freedom, he indwells it. This is the meaning of the doctrine of merit, which has so often caused misunderstanding: it means that we can quite truly be said to be the source of our own supernatural actions. Not that we are their ultimate source, but that they proceed by way of our freedom.

Our Lord gives us an illustration of this in the parable of the talents *(Mt 25:14ff)*. The master, when he sets off on his journey, simply entrusts his money to the servants; he does not give them precise instructions as to what they are to do with it. It is up to them to trade, with all the risks involved. It is up to us to make something of the gift that God has given to us. The Holy Spirit is given to us to be the source of actions that will be authentically and freely *ours*.

The precise relationship between our freedom and God's grace is one of the theological problems that has never been satisfactorily cleared up, and we must remember in all this discussion that we are using images, models, pictures that have a certain degree of applicability, but need to be complemented always by other images and models. But it does seem clear that docility to God cannot adequately be interpreted just as rubrical correctness or a kind of mathematical accuracy. It is more like a poet wrestling with language, feeling his way towards the right word. This is totally different from the school-boy trying to remember the right word for sausage in French. It is a creative rightness. Man is made in the image of his creator, so man too is meant to be a creator, he must develop a creative sense of rightness, like that of the painter or composer, who never has or could have any external guarantee of the rightness of his work. There is no "right answer" at the back of the book to assure him that he is right.

Unlearning the false "creativity" of original sin, we must learn true creativity, if we would keep company with him who is the creator of all. A fussy, pedantic approach to life will not fit us for the friendship of God's sublime and infinite freedom.

We must not be too concerned with the "materiality" of the Christian life,[83] with doing this and not doing that. At best that will only touch the surface of it. At times it may indeed be the best we can muster, at times it may be the most sensible and practical way to proceed—at times when we are deeply confused, for instance, it is common sense to adhere to a regular pattern of life. But eventually God calls us to be free as the wind, blowing inscrutably and unpredictably where it will. "Such are those who are born of the Spirit" (Jn 3:8).

It is a matter of becoming a certain kind of person, sufficiently attuned to God's ways, to God's tastes, to be able to enjoy the unbounded, uninhibited company of God, who is his own life, conditioned and determined by nothing except himself.

The question of freedom, then, is very important for our life of prayer. It is important both in connexion with our picture of Christian maturity, and in connexion with our growth towards that maturity. We must grow towards a kind of freedom which is very much more than that of the slogan-mongers, a freedom which is the fruit of charity and docility to the Holy Spirit. But if we are to grow towards such freedom, we must already be free to grow.

All too often we seem to think that we are required to be perfect all at once, as if we could step out of our sins and all the moral and psychological consequences of sin, straight into perfect holiness, with no intervening period of growth. That is not what St Paul says! He actually defines Christian perfection in terms of constantly pressing on, not turning back to what lies behind, trying not to sink below whatever level one has attained, and always reaching out to what lies ahead *(Phil 3:12–16)*.

Once again the psychology of adolescence can shed some light on the matter. Frightened by the vastness of the new world opening out within him and around him, the adolescent who, of course, has hardly any real experience to guide him, is often tempted to adopt a stance as if he had already explored everything and discovered all the answers. It is at first sight considerably easier than actually doing the exploring, the growing; but this assumption of competence and maturity, in so far as it succeeds, actually prevents any real growth towards true competence and maturity.

The spiritual equivalent of this is to assume that conversion is something that basically takes place all at once. There may be a bit of mopping up to be done, and occasional lapses may still occur, but basically, one might think, one has arrived. But nothing could be further from the truth. When the Bible says categorically that we have been saved, that refers to the objective fact of God's attitude to us, not to our subjective appropriation of his grace. So the Bible also says, with great caution, "Work out your salvation with fear and trembling" *(Phil 2:12)*. St Paul addresses himself to "those who are in process of being saved" (e.g. *1 Cor 1:18*; the unambiguous present participle in the Greek is often disguised in the versions). God's act is decisive; but its effect in us is a long process of growth. The seed that tries to grow too quickly, dies because it has no roots *(Mt 13:5f)*.

Of course as soon as we come to Christ we are confronted with the whole of the Gospel; but we must not assume that we can immediately bring our lives into full conformity with it, or even that we shall see all at once exactly what demands it actually makes upon us. There will be enormous tangles of old habits to be worked through. We must not assume that somehow we *ought* to be able to become perfect at once, if only we had enough will power or enough faith. It is precisely by the long processes of growth that our will becomes truly strong and healthy and our faith becomes more total and simple. We may remember that St Irenaeus regards the Fall as occurring precisely because man was in too much of a hurry and refused to take time to grow up. Of course we must confess before God that all is not as it should be, and we must have some purpose of amendment, but it must be a realistic one. We might even say that it must have an eschatological dimension to it: we hope that at the end, by the power of Christ, we shall indeed be made perfect, perfectly converted to the will and the ways of God from the depth of our heart. We must also be resolved, in so far as we can, never to refuse any grace that is offered to us for our growth in Christ. But then we must recognise that there is still going to be an awful amount in our situation that is not, as yet, directly affected by our new life.

Two images can perhaps help us to see the point. Sin is a miry bog into which we have fallen, and from which we desire to be rescued. But "the waters have come up to my neck" *(Ps 68 (69):2)*. The way out from that muddy condition is through a lot of mud. Being rescued from a swamp is a messy business. We must aspire in the right direction, but we should not presume that we have got further than we have; we must be patient with the process of redemption.

Indeed, as we are pulled clear of the mud, we shall be able to see further, and so we may actually discover that there is more mud than we had thought. For instance, looking back over our lives we may often discover that things that had seemed quite in order at the time, seen from our present vantage point, are clearly wrong. This is one reason why the Church lets us make general confessions: it is not strictly that such unnoticed sins in our past are unforgiven, but the discovery of such sins can be an oppressive burden for our conscience, which can be handed over to the Lord in this way.

Another picture of sin is that it is a great block of ice, frozen solid in the coldness of separation from God. When God's warmth invades it, it begins to melt. But it does not melt all at once. At any given moment, we must be prepared to put up with the fact that a great deal of it is still frozen solid. There may be very real aspects of my situation that are objectively wrong. There may be relationships which are unChristian, relationships of bitterness, hatred, possessiveness, which I know to be wrong, but cannot, so far, do anything about—except perhaps, at my best, regret them. Rather than being disheartened by all this, we should rejoice that the Lord is at work, rejoice in whatever does seem to be melting, even if it is only a very small improvement. Much of the Lord's work will be below the level of consciousness in any case, so we must not be too insistent on wanting to know everything that he is up to. He is not answerable to us.

Surely the most important thing for us is to keep our eyes open and learn from all our experience how to make the best use of our actual opportunities. This means that we must recognise our situation for what it is, and know what resources we have to draw on.

A very dangerous misconception of freedom is to regard it as a situation totally devoid of obstacles or limitations of any kind. That would not be human freedom. For us freedom is always freedom within a particular context. If I want to be free in my room, for instance, I must respect the shape of the room, the distribution of the furniture, and so on. If I am sitting at my table and want to get to the other side of it, there are all kinds of possibilities open to me : I may climb over it, or under it, I may leapfrog over it, or I may move the table. I may even, in a prosaic mood, just walk round it. But I cannot walk through it as if it were not there. I must respect my situation. And I must respect my resources too. If I were a bird I could fly over the table. If I have broken both my legs, that changes the picture considerably, probably ruling out all the methods suggested above. I might have to call for help. But if, having broken both my legs, I had also acquired a wheelchair, that again would change the picture.

We must learn to live in our actual situation, with our actual resources; and that is of course something constantly shifting : our situation in life is always evolving, and our resources are often erratic. We must keep our eyes open, and not presume that we know it all already. Every now and then someone will perhaps pay a big cheque into my account, and I shall be able to forgive someone against whom I had cherished resentment for fourteen years, or smile at old aunty when she is at her most importunate and inconvenient. But then sometimes the pound drops, and my easy, comfortable devotional life will suddenly be beyond my means. One day we may have faith to move mountains, and find ourselves the next day scarcely able to get above twiddling our thumbs hoping nothing is going to happen.

We must be free to grow, and that means being free to be realistic about ourselves and our situation, accepting both as they become apparent and not insisting on knowing more than we do know, nor wasting energy regretting that we have not got better resources than we have got. After all, the only way to improve our resources is by making good use of what we have got.

This way we shall discover, in the most solid and practical way, that the initiative is not, in the last analysis, ours. We shall find ourselves therefore living in a world in which we are not God. It will therefore become possible and may even become imperative to pray to a God who is other than ourselves.

And we shall be reminded of this over and over again. Often we shall be tempted to think that at last we have begun to see the pattern, at last we are beginning to find our way around, or at last we have mastered whatever lesson was being taught us. And then, without warning, we shall be moved into the next class and have to start all over again at the bottom.

And progress is not likely to occur in a straight line. Our Lord is concerned to make us fully alive, with hearts fully human and fully responsive to him.

E

And so he uses all kinds of different situations to give us a chance to discover different aspects of life, different facets of faith and hope and love, learning to recognise his presence in a hundred and one different ways. Over and over again we shall have to drop, humbly and simply, our pretended insight and limited expectations, to surrender to his formation.

In her marvellous book, *A Wizard of Earthsea*,[84] Ursula le Guin shows us the young Sparrowhawk, with his first smattering of village witchcraft, going off on his first journey with the great mage Ogion. Nothing seemed to be happening. At last the boy approached his master : " 'When will my apprenticeship begin, Sir?' 'It has begun,' said Ogion. 'But I haven't learned anything yet!' 'Because you haven't found out what I am teaching,' replied the mage, going on at his steady, long-legged pace along their road".

So often we are too full of what we think should be happening to us in our spiritual formation to notice what God is actually teaching us. We must be still enough, simple enough, humble enough, to let him plan the course, and use whatever opportunities there may be for our instruction.

We must not think that as we progress in prayer everything will necessarily become much more overtly holy. What it will become is more simple, more humble, more actual.

St Ambrose gave his congregation some very good advice. Using the old Christian symbol, he compared them in this stormy world to fish swimming in the sea. And to them too he said: "Be a fish".[85] We must learn how not to be swamped by the situations that we find ourselves in. We must learn how to get through them with a minimum of damage, and a maximum of profit.

One aspect of this is simply learning to get through situations, and not always to want to take them with us. There is a story told of two monks in Japan, "travelling together down a muddy road. A heavy rain was still falling. Coming around a bend, they met a lovely girl in a silk kimono and sash, unable to cross the intersection. 'Come on, girl,' said Tanzan at once. Lifting her in his arms, he carried her over the mud. Ekido did not speak again until that night when they reached a lodging temple. Then he no longer could restrain himself. 'We monks don't go near females,' he told Tanzan, 'especially not young and lovely ones. It is dangerous. Why did you do that?' 'I left the girl there,' said Tanzan. 'Are you still carrying her?' "[86]

We must learn to pass through situations like a fish, rather than carrying them all with us like a snail. We should certainly emerge with a little bit more experience of life, but there is no need to carry more with us than we have to—each situation carries quite enough trouble with it by itself!

Again, we should not be too ambitious. How we love doing good! Yet surely it is often sheer vanity to think that we can do good. The old Christians regarded it as a marvellous thing if they could manage not to do harm. They aspired first of all simply to innocence, harmlessness.[87] They knew what dangerous beasts we are. If they could actually help someone, that was God's business; for themselves, they just wanted and hoped to get through life doing as little harm as possible.

We must learn to be very simple and resigned, accepting life as it comes, seeking to build up an instinct for what God is trying to teach us day by day, trying to become more sensitive to the fluctuating state of our inner and outer resources, and not grumbling to find that we are poor.

Indeed, "blessed are the poor" *(Mt 5:3)*. And it is the poor who know how to pray. William Peraldus says that we can only pray empty-handed.[88] If we want to pray, we must learn how to be empty-handed.

And then we shall find, even in our imperfections and weaknesses, that already we are beginning to live in God's world, and so already we shall be able to begin, rather shyly, to keep company with him.

And he will lead us to our goal.

10 "My God and My All"

*What else is there for a wise and perfect man
to do, except to play, to hold festival with God?*
Clement of Alexandria[89]

*I'm Nobody! Who are you?
Are you—Nobody—too?
Then there's a pair of us!
Don't tell! they'd advertise—you know!*
Emily Dickinson[90]

"What could be greedier," remarks St Augustine, "than a man for whom God is not enough?"[91] Yet how hard it is for us to be really satisfied with God! It is only one who has learned how to be poor and simple who can really say in all sincerity "my God and my all", the prayer which St Francis is said to have used all night long on occasion.[92]

The psalmist, wrestling with the difficulties of life, tempted to cynicism by seeing how it is the arrogant and impious who succeed in this world, describes how it was in the very experience of bitterness and despair that he began to discover what it was all about *(Ps 72/73)* :

> And so when my heart grew embittered
> and when I was cut to the quick,
> I was stupid and did not understand,
> no better than a beast in your sight.

119

Yet I was always in your presence;
you were holding me by my right hand.
You will guide me by your counsel
and so you will lead me to glory.
What else have I in heaven but you?
Apart from you I want nothing on earth.
My body and my heart faint for joy;
God is my possession for ever.

Grail

This doctrine of the entire sufficiency of God is
perhaps one of the greatest stumbling blocks for man.
Yet if we would find our true bliss in God we must,
by keeping company with him even in the darkness
of despair and incomprehension, learn what kind of
a God he is, and what kind of joy he has and has to
share.

And it is in fact the very perfection of charity to
come to this sympathy and generosity. In his last dis-
course, in St John's gospel, our Lord tells his disciples
that if they really loved him they would rejoice at his
going to the Father who is greater than he, who is the
source of all that he is (Jn 14:28). Because they have
not yet really understood what it means to love him,
they want to hold on to him, like Mary in the garden
(Jn 20:17). And like her they have to learn not to
hold on, but to let him go to his Father, and indeed
to rejoice in his going.

Our Lord himself indicates what a stumbling
block this is to us. After his declaration that his body
and blood are the food and drink that give life,
many of his followers are too shocked to go on. But
Jesus only comments: "Does that shock you? What

if you should see the Son of Man ascending where he was before?" *(Jn 6:60ff)*.

This mystery is shocking above all others because it reminds us so forcibly and intransigently that the life which Christ brings us, the life of fellowship with God, does not consist in our drawing God into our world, but in his drawing us into his world. The doorway for us is simply that Christ the Son of God is one with his Father. Because he lives, we live (cf. *Jn 14:19)*; because he lives with his Father, our life too is hidden with him in God *(Col 3:3)*. He calls himself a burglar, and it is not only the devil who has been burgled : he has stolen us from ourselves, we no longer belong to ourselves.

If we would truly pray, we must respect this law of the spiritual life, that the direction is upwards *(cf. Col 3:1f)*. Its centre is not us in our world, but God in his.

St James puts it with his usual bluntness*(4:1ff)* : "Why are there wars and battles among you? Is it not because of your selfish pleasures which are themselves at war in your bodies? You desire and do not have, so you murder; you are jealous and do not get what you want, so you fight and go to war. You do not possess, because you do not ask; if you do ask, you do not receive, because you ask badly, simply to squander everything on your selfish pleasures. Harlots! Do you not know that friendship with the world is enmity with God?"

Our prayer will be futile if we are seeking simply to draw God into our own selfish schemes. And of course that does not only apply to obviously sinful schemes. I should not invoke God's aid upon my plans for murder or theft, but equally wrong is the attempt to exploit God in the interests of my own moral goodness. John V. Taylor in his book, *The Go-between God,* laments that many people want to be good, but not many people want God.[93] Of course really wanting God entails the desire to be good; but God is not just the means by which I become good. Rather, goodness is an integral—but not focal—aspect of my seeking to be one with God.

Incidentally I think we should occasionally scrutinise our own praying to see just what we mean when we say, "Please God, help me to do . . ." Of course this can be a perfectly legitimate way of praying, and it has ample support in scripture and in the liturgy. But if it simply means that we decide what is to be done and then require God to provide, as it were, the supernatural fuel, then surely we have sadly missed the point. We are meant to become part of God's schemes, not to make him part of ours.

Related to this is the hoary problem of why an omnipotent and loving God permits so much evil and suffering to go on in the world. This is not the place to go into all the deep and difficult theological and philosophical issues involved; but we must notice how easily we ask this question in a way which assumes that we have the right to tell God what he ought to be doing. But the Bible warns us very severely against "putting the Lord to the test" *(Deut 6:16).* He is not a candidate for an examination that we have set. God is not subject to our specifications, and if we want to live in relationship with him we must begin by letting him be according to his own specifications.

There is a further misconception too about omnipotence. It is assumed that if God is omnipotent he can do anything; but this is not strictly true. What God's omnipotence does mean is that nothing can obstruct him, nothing can prevent his being fully and eternally himself.

But this means that it is actually a part of his omnipotence that God does not contradict himself. He is free to determine the manner of his own working; and in fact, as we know from revelation, he has chosen to work in such a way that we can interfere, and interfere very drastically, with his creation. God made man such that man could rebel against him, and set up his own "world" in opposition to God. Of course, God is not without allies even in "our" world; he knows that we can never really be satisfied with any world of our own devising, so that it will always be vulnerable to his influence in one way or another; and God exploits this to the full. But he always respects the freedom and independence that he has given us.

This is why the early Christians loved to say that God did not redeem man by an autocratic *fiat*, but by coming and tricking the devil, so that the devil, having bitten off more than he could digest, had himself to vomit back into the light of God's day those whom he had swallowed into darkness.[94]

Before we get too carried away with thoughts of God's power, we should listen attentively to what St Paul says about the "weakness of God" *(1 Cor 1:25)*, which is a vital part of God's self-revelation. If we look at the way in which he discloses himself in Jesus Christ we have to acknowledge that he does not come into our world with a great display of superior power; in fact, this was one of the temptations which our Lord had to resist as being contrary to his mission, contrary to his true nature *(Mt 4:5ff)*. He does not come in strength but in weakness, and he chooses the foolish and weak and unimportant things of the world, things that are nothing at all, to overthrow the strength and impressiveness of the world. As we saw earlier, he is like the judo expert who uses the strength of his opponent to bring him to the ground; it is the art of self-defence proper to the weak.

This is why, if we keep clamouring for things we want from God, we may often find ourselves disappointed, because we have forgotten the weakness of God and what we may call the poverty of God. We had thought of God as the dispenser of all the good things we would possibly desire; but in a very real sense, God has nothing to give at all except himself.

Of course, if we let God give himself, then everything does become different, and this may be dramatically symbolised in an outward change in our circumstances. There are miracles in the Gospels. But the miracles are essentially signs, and if we will not see them as signs, we shall miss the point. If what God was primarily interested in was healing the sick, then he made a thoroughly bad job of it. For every one or two healed, he left millions unhealed. The healing miracles were signs of God giving himself in the intensity of his own life, against which sickness cannot stand any more than sin can—and in the Gospel it is noticeable that bodily healing is often a sign of that spiritual healing which is forgiveness. But even that is really only a sign; as we have seen, there can be a wrong approach to forgiveness which obscures its true nature.

Even the apostles, it seems, had not grasped what Jesus was really doing; even after the resurrection they still thought that if he was really the Messiah, it was about time he started overthrowing the Romans *(Acts 1:6)*. It was only at Pentecost that they suddenly realised that what he was doing was essentially giving himself, giving his own life, giving his own Spirit. That is the gift that he has to give us *(cf. Lk 11:13)*. If we forget that, if we forget the poverty of God, then we shall keep demanding everything except the one thing that he has got to give us, and so our whole prayer life, our whole Christian life, will be off key. Whatever our problem is, whatever the anxiety we bring to the Lord, he has got only one thing to say, only one answer : himself.

The Bible gives us a glimpse into the great mystery of God's self-revelation in Jesus Christ : it tells us that in Jesus Christ God utters in human flesh that Word in which he utters his own divine fullness, the one and only Word that God has to speak, and

which he speaks from all eternity to all eternity
(Jn 1; Col 2:9).

This was already intimated obscurely at the
beginning of the Exodus, that pattern for all God's
redemptive activity. When Moses wants to know
God's credentials, so that he will know what to tell
the people, the only answer he gets is that enigmatic
"I am who I am". One can almost hear God saying,
"So there!" If people will not take that, there is
nothing more to be said about it. Redemption comes
about essentially through God's utterance of himself,
without qualification or limit.

And in all this there is a deep harmony between
redemption and creation. It is in God's Word that
all things are created. Our fear of confusing God
with creation must not lead us to posit too absolute
a break between them. St Thomas in one of his
minor works[95] asks explicitly whether God has more
than one thing to say, one Word in which he utters
himself, and a different word in which he produces
creatures. And he answers "No". God has only one
thing to say. It is within his utterance of himself that
all things are made.

The only solution that God has to offer to all our
problems is himself, is the fact that he is, that he is
the kind of God that he is, a God who has a Word
to utter, which he utters in an ecstasy of joy, an
ecstasy of giving, which we call the Holy Spirit.

Of course he is the solution to all our problems,
but it is a solution that requires that we should look
in the right direction. In one sense God is not

answering our questions or solving our problem at all; we might even say that he is rather questioning our answers, questioning even our questioning. He is challenging us to see it all in a different light, to discover the question, which is no question, to which he is the answer. As long as we are preoccupied with our questions, we shall not appreciate that God has answered and answered definitively, and so of course we shall go on complaining that he is not doing this, he has not done that, why doesn't he do this? We shall be like the boy in Ursula le Guin's story, learning nothing, hearing nothing, because we have not discovered what is being taught, what is being said.

God has only the one thing to say, which is himself, he has only the one thing to give, which is himself. And he invites us to hear that Word, to treasure it in our hearts and find in it the source of all our bliss. He wants us, quite precisely, to enter into the joy of our Lord *(Mt 25:21)*. In St John's gospel one feels sometimes a kind of frustration in our Lord, longing so intensely to share everything with his friends, so that his own joy might be in them, and their joy be full *(Jn 15:11)*. But they kept clamouring for something else. Even their most pious aspirations were a bit off course. "Show us the Father," they cried, "then we shall be content." "Haven't you yet realised," he had to ask them, "he who has seen me has seen the Father?" *(Jn 14:8ff)*. Somehow they thought that God must have something more up his sleeve, something more impressively divine, a God who would pass their test in divinity.

This is certainly not to say that there is no more to God than the humanity of Jesus. But it does mean that we must accept that God is the kind of God who, if he wants to show himself in our world, must do so in weakness and poverty.

That is why he says, "Blessed are the poor". The poor are blessed because they are like God, and so can sympathise with him, recognise what he is saying, accept what he is giving, and find in that their joy. And this is a joy that cannot be taken away from them, because it is a joy that does not rest on any of the precarious circumstances of this world: it rests secure in the impregnable nature of God himself, giving himself, being himself. He *is* love, he cannot help giving himself; that is the very life of God, the Father giving himself to the Son, the Son not clutching that gift to himself *(cf. Phil 2:6)* but returning it to the Father, so that from that interchange comes the Holy Spirit whose name is Gift. There is nothing in God that is not giving and given.

There is a lovely story in the Gospel which illustrates this *(Mk 12:41ff)*. Our Lord is sitting by the Temple watching all the people coming and going, putting their offerings into the box. Some of them were making quite a show of it, no doubt, so that everyone would know how much they had put in. But there, among them all, was a little old lady, rather shabbily dressed, who slipped in her twopence halfpenny when no one was looking. But the Lord saw her. And he got terribly excited about it. "She's put in more than all the rest put together!" he exclaims.

This little old lady did not realise that she was doing anything spectacular; nothing could have been further from her mind. She did not want to draw attention to herself, because she knew that what she was giving was not worth very much, it was not going to repair the Temple roof or get them a new organ or even pay for the Boy Scouts' Annual Outing. The Temple authorities might well think it was a confounded nuisance having to count all the small change put in by people like her. But she had given all she had, knowing that it was not much, knowing that she was not going to solve anyone's problems. And surely the Lord recognised in her a kindred spirit. She was doing the same kind of thing that he was doing. He was not solving the world's problems in any sense that the world could understand, he was not reforming society or abolishing poverty—"the poor you will always have with you" was his comment on that (Mt 26:11)—he was not doing any of the things some modern Christians think he should have been doing. And many people considered him a nuisance. But he was giving himself, he was giving all he had got, he was giving his very life.

Blessed are the poor! How easily we take that always to mean somebody else. Yet if we want to be with God, we must learn to hear it as "blessed are we who are poor", we who have not got anything very impressive to give to anybody, whose giving may very well be rather a nuisance, but who still have not given up giving. Who knows? Our giving of ourselves in all our poverty may one day bring some joy to somebody else who is poor, who is not calculating, not trying to repair a church roof. God invites us into this conspiracy of the poor, making himself its head, giving himself in poverty and weakness, knowing that if we will only receive that humble gift of his, it will transform everything. If we are prepared to be poor enough to learn and to appreciate the manner of God's giving, we shall find in that poverty the seed of all perfection.

And so we shall find, mysteriously, that this unobtrusive and unimpressive gift in which God simply gives himself, is the seed of that final revelation of glory when every tear will be wiped away and all pain and sickness and misery banished. The only way to that fullness is through that smallness, otherwise we shall miss the point even of the final bliss. When our Lord tells us to seek first the kingdom of God, and then everything else will be added (Mt 6:33), he does not mean—as he has unfortunately sometimes been taken to mean—that piety is the way to prosperity ("prayer pays"), but that when God is all in all, then automatically "All shall be well, and all shall be well, and all manner thing shall be well".[96] That is what it means for all to be well.

We are not invited to be smug about suffering and injustice and want; we should long for the final abolition of all evil. But we should realise what that means: it means the final establishment of God's kingdom in all its fullness, and that means the definite utterance in all creation of God's own Word, so that he who is all fullness may indeed fill all things. Short of that, we must, in all compassion, recognise that the Gospel is not a way of patching up this world. God has never promised that if only we have enough faith, if only we pray enough, all problems will disappear. Our prayer must always be, at least implicitly, "Thy kingdom come". The resurrection of our Lord does not mean that our world is no longer heading for death and decay; it means that death does not have the last word. The new world will be born out of the death of this one, and it will be born through the triumphant utterance of God's one and only Word, in whom already we share in the life without end.

So we must respect the law of God's giving, letting him give what he does have to give, himself. And the more we penetrate the simplicity of that gift, the more we shall find there all sweetness and all joy. We shall find, with infinite amazement and gratitude, that there is the peace which our Lord promised to us, a peace not given in the way the world gives, but a peace that is precisely himself *(Eph 2:14)*. This peace, this joy, can never be shattered because its foundation is in God's own infinite joy and peace. If we really loved him, then that of itself would be the fullness of joy for us, that God is God, that the Son is with the Father in the unity of the Holy Spirit. May he free us from ourselves, from the blindness of our own pre-occupations, so that our hearts, even in the midst of all the pain and weariness of life in this world, may rise up to him in simple faith and generosity, to receive from him the essential gift which is himself. Amen.

Notes

The notes contain some details concerning the quotations and references made in the text. There is no additional matter to be found here, and most people should probably ignore the notes altogether.

1. Clement of Alexandria, *Strom.* VII 7, 39, 6; Evagrius Ponticus, *de Or.* 3. Other references in Lampe, Patristic Greek Lexicon s.v. *euché* IBi.
2. Murder in the Cathedral, Part ii, line 257.
3. Orthodoxy (Fontana paperback) pp. 65f.
4. Gregory of Sinai, Texts on Commandments and Dogmas, 113. (PG 150:1277); ET in Writings from the Philokalia on Prayer of the Heart, trans. E. Kadloubovsky and G. E. H. Palmer (Faber and Faber 1951) p. 62.
5. Cf. The Way of a Pilgrim, trans. R. M. French (S.P.C.K.), p. 47.
6. Evans-Wentz, Tibetan Yoga (O.U.P.). Precepts of the Gurus, I x, 1.
7. Letter 91 (Chitty)=90 (Solesmes)=185 (Volos).
8. Apophthegmata Patrum, Nau 65. (Revue de l'Orient Chrétien, 1907). French trans. in Les Sentences des Pères du Désert, Nouveau Receuil. (Solesmes, 1970).
9. Cf. Douglas Gray, Themes and Images in the Medieval English Religious Lyric (London, 1972), pp. 38ff, especially the poem on p. 40. See also Frances Yates, The Art of Memory (Peregrine Books 1966), pp. 18ff.
10. Vergil, *Ecl.* I 2.
11. Cf. Augustine, *de Doctr. Christiana* II 12; 14.
12. Cf. Y. Congar, Tradition and the Life of the Church (Fact & Faith), p. 22.
13. IIa IIae q. 1 a.2.
14. "you shall above all things be glad and young" and "may my heart always be open to little" (e. e. cummings, selected poems, Penguin Books, pp. 40 & 39).

15. *De Eruditione Religiosorum* I ch. 2 (published in Maxima Bibliotheca Veterum Patrum, Lyon 1677, vol. 25, under the name of Humbert of Romans).
16. Orthodoxy, p. 59 (see Note 3).
17. "This was a Poet" (Poems no. 448).
18. Orthodoxy, p. 53 (see Note 3).
19. *In Evang. Ioh.*, tr. 8, 1.
20. Hymn by Eleanor Farjeon (in Kevin Mayhew's 20th Century Folk Hymnal, 1974).
21. Orthodoxy, pp. 53f (see Note 3).
22. Celestial Hierarchies, 3.
23. Letters to Malcolm (Fontana paperback) p. 23.
24. See Arthur Vööbus, History of Asceticism in the Syrian Orient, vol. II (Louvain, 1960), pp. 49f.
25. *Cat. Magn.* I 11 (I have taken this reference from Théologie de la Vie Monastique (Aubier, 1961), p. 428.)
26. *Protr.* X 93, 2.
27. Dialogue ch. 165.
28. Hermas, *Sim.* IX 32, (109).
29. A ladder of four rungs (in Deonise Hid Divinite, ed. Phyllis Hodgson, Early English Text Society 231), pp 113f.
30. The Koran, trans. Arthur J. Arberry (O.U.P., World's Classics), p. 45.
31. See The Jerome Biblical Commentary, and von Rad: Genesis, ad loc.
32. Ia q. 14 a. 4.
33 *De Trin.* XV 13, 22.
34. *Adv. Haer.* IV 38; *Dem. Apost.* 12ff.
35. Ginzberg, Legends of the Jews, vol. I, p. 59.
36. R. Sennett, The Uses of Disorder (Pelican books), ch. 1 and 2.
37. Cf. the Collect for the 13th week of the year in the new Missal.
38. The Hound of Heaven.
39. Where Silence is Praise (Darton Longman & Todd), p. 102.
40. *Ad Eph.* 8, 2.
41. *Contra Gentiles* IV 55; cf. IIa IIae q. 161 a. 1 ad 3.
42. Chapter 2.
43. " God made a little Gentian" (Poems no. 442).
44. Meditations (ed. André Wilmart, Paris, 1936), 204. There is an ET by J. J. Jolin (Milwaukee, 1951).
45. Unfortunately I have mislaid the reference.
46. Don Marquis, Archy and Mehitabel: the lesson of the moth.

47. Apophthegmata Patrum, Alonius 2 (PG 65 : 133).
48. Ibid. Pambo 10 (PG 65:372).
49. Ia IIae q. 17 a. 7.
50. Orthodoxy, p. 19 (see Note 3).
51. Phaedrus 246ff.
52. The Great Divorce (Fontana paperback) pp. 89ff.
53. Cf. St Thomas, Ia q. 98 a. 2 ad 3.
54. IIa IIae q. 155 a. 4
55. Ia q.81 a.2.
56. Cf. Evagrius Ponticus, Pract. 24; ad Eulog. 10 (PG 79 : 1105).
57. William Blatty, The Exorcist (Corgi paperback) pp. 308ff.
58. R. Murray, Symbols of Church and Kingdom in the Early Syriac Fathers (to be published in 1975 by Cambridge). I am most grateful to Fr Murray for letting me see his type-script; I am indebted to him for several ancient references.
59. Athanasius, Life of Anthony, 13.
60. Vööbus, History of Asceticism, II p. 215 (see Note 24), with a citation from Severus of Antioch.
61. Cf. Ia q. 81 a. 2.
62. Meditations (see Note 44) no. 119.
63. Cf. Evagrius Ponticus, Pract. 38.
64. G. K. Chesterton, The Secret of Father Brown (Penguin paperback), pp. 11f. Cf. Vincent Ferrer, de Vita Spir. ch. 4 (ed. Fages, Paris, 1909).
65. The Nine Ways of Prayer of St Dominic (Analecta O.P. XV (1922) pp. 93ff), 2nd way.
66. Postcommunion prayer for Whit-Tuesday in the old Missal.
67. Tretyse of Loue, ed. John H. Fisher (E.E.T.S. 223) p. 79.
68. De Grad. Hum. ch. 5.
69. Don Marquis, Archy and Mehitabel : the lesson of the moth.
70. Cf. St Thomas Contra Gentiles III 17ff.
71. De Div. Nom. ch. 4 (PG 2:709-713).
72. E.g. Vincent Ferrer, de Vita Spir. especially chapters 3 and 5 (Fages. See Note 64.).
73. Screwtape Letters, XVII.
74. Surprised by Joy; Pilgrim's Regress.
75. Cántico Espiritual, can. 4 & 5. The idea comes from Augustine, Conf. X vi.
76. Letter 16.
77. Summa de Virtutibus. I quote page numbers from the edition published in Paris, 1519. p. clxxxi r (b).
78. The Little Prince, trans. Katherine Woods, chapter 9.

79. *In I Ep. Ioh.*, tr. 7, 8.
80. Gifts of the Holy Ghost, I 5. There is a rather unsatisfactory ET by Dominic Hughes, London, 1951.
81. Postcommunion prayer of the Mass for Peace in the old Missal.
82. Ia IIae Prol.
83. Cf. J. G. Arintero, O.P., *La Evolución Mística* I iii 1. ET by Jordan Aumann, O.P.: The Mystical Evolution in the Development and Vitality of the Church (Herder, 1949).
84. A Wizard of Earthsea (Puffin paperback) p. 28.
85. *De Sacr.* III 3, 3.
86. *Zen Flesh, Zen Bones,* compiled by Paul Reps : Zen Stories, 14.
87. Apophthegmata Patrum, Poemen 159 (PG 65:361); cf. Lactantius, *Epitome* 60 (PL 6:1070); Aelred, *Inst. Inclusarum* 27.
88. *De Virtutibus,* p. clxxix r (b) (see Note 77).
89. *Paed.* I v 22, 1.
90. "I'm Nobody!" (Poems no. 288).
91. *In I Ep. Ioh.*, tr. 8, 6.
92. *Legenda Trium Sociorum* 28.
93. John V. Taylor, The Go-between God (London 1972).
94. Cf. George Every, Christian Mythology (London, 1970), pp. 65ff.
95. *Quodl.* IV q. 4 a. 6.
96. Julian of Norwich, ch. 27.

Persons and Sources

AELRED OF RIEVAULX, St. 1109-67. Famous English Cistercian writer; friend of St Bernard. See Aelred of Rievaulx, by Aelred Squire (London 1969).

ALEXANDER AKOIMETES. A wandering monk of the eastern Church. Died c. 430. Although by his time, his kind of monasticism was not in favour with Church authorities, he embodies a very traditional kind of Syrian asceticism, and at least one of his followers was canonised.

AMBROSE, St. c. 339-97. Bishop of Milan, doctor of the Church.

ANSELM, St. c. 1033-1109. Archbishop of Canterbury. His Meditations had a considerable effect on medieval piety.

ANTHONY the GREAT, St. c. 269. He became a solitary in the Egyptian desert; he is regarded as the Father of Monks. The Life by St Athanasius soon became a spiritual classic, and was one factor in the conversion of St Augustine.

APOPHTHEGMATA PATRUM. Collections of sayings and doings of the old monks, the Desert Fathers. They form a marvellous source of monastic "case law". Helen Waddell, The Desert Fathers, gives a selection in English translation (Fontana paperback).

ARINTERO, J. G. Dominican theologian and spiritual director, who taught at Salamanca. 1860-1928. He was one of the pioneers of the revival of mystical theology as a serious part of theology.

ATHANASIUS, St. Bishop of Alexandria, friend of the Egyptian monks. c. 296-373. Doctor of the Church.

AUGUSTINE of HIPPO, St. Bishop of Hippo (in what is now Algeria). 354-430. His autobiographical Confessions became a classic. Doctor of the Church.

BAKER, Father AUGUSTINE. English Benedictine monk and spiritual writer. 1575-1641. His Holy Wisdom enjoyed long popularity.

BARSANUPHIUS, St. Died c. 543. An Egyptian who lived as a recluse in Gaza, communicating with his numerous disciples through an intermediary in letters, many of which survive, and which are masterpieces of spiritual direction.

BENEDICT, St. c.480-c.550. Father of western monasticism. His Rule is the basic document for all western monks.

BERNARD, St. 1090-1153. Abbot of the Cistercian monastery of Clairvaux, he is the best known of all the Cistercian Fathers, and is regarded as the last of the Fathers of the Church. His Sermons on the Song of Songs are a spiritual classic, as is his treatise on the Steps of Humility.

CASSIAN, St JOHN. The interpreter of eastern monasticism to the Latin west, he eventually settled in Marseilles. c. 360-c. 430. He was a friend of Pope Leo I and enjoyed great authority in his own day, and became the standard spiritual reading of western monks, a position he held well into the middle ages. His sanctity, though not widely celebrated, is undoubted and has been officially recognised.

CATHARINUS, AMBROSIUS. c. 1484-1553. A controversial Dominican theologian, who fell out with the scholastic orthodoxy of his day, but was in high standing with the Papal court. He was one of the papal theologians at the Council of Trent. The most detailed and sympathetic account of his work is the article on him by M. M. Gorce in Dictionnaire de Théologie Catholique XII 2418ff.

CATHERINE of SIENA, St. Dominican sister. 1347-1380. She was a great mystic and spiritual teacher, as well as playing a very public part in the affairs of her time. She was declared a doctor of the Church in 1970.

CLEMENT OF ALEXANDRIA. c.150-c.215. One of the first Christian humanists. He was for a long time regarded as a saint.

CLOUD OF UNKNOWING. A well-known anonymous mystical treatise written in English in the fourteenth century.

CURÉ d'ARS (St John Mary Vianney). Unlettered parish priest in France, who became one of the most famous priests in Europe, whose confessional was filled with penitents day and night from far and wide. 1786-1859.

DIDACHE. An ancient book of Christian instructions, possibly dating from the 1st century.

DIONYSIUS (Pseudo—). c. 500. Some eastern Christian produced a corpus of highly obscure but very important mystical, theological writings, which he placed under the name of Dionysius the Areopagite, thus claiming for them almost apostolic authority. They were rapidly taken up as a major authority, especially in the western Church.

DOMINIC, St. Born in the north of Spain in 1170, he became a Canon, and then founded the Order of Preachers in 1221, shortly before he died. He was a man of immense charm, and great breadth of vision and compassion. Contrary to the previous tradition of religious life, he believed in the virtue of laughter. On the occasion of the centenary celebrations in Rome in 1970, Cardinal Villot described him as a man who was "stupefyingly free".

ECKHART, Meister. c. 1260-1327. German Dominican theologian and mystic. He enjoyed great fame as a spiritual director, but his daring language got him into trouble with ecclesiastical authority; the orthodoxy of his intentions is not in doubt, even though he has been claimed by some as a forerunner of all kinds of odd doctrines.

EPHREM, St. The most famous luminary of the Syriac Church. Died 373. He was a monk, a scholar, and one of the great religious poets of the world.

EUSEBIUS. Bishop of Caesarea, and the first Church historian c.260-c.340.

EVAGRIUS PONTICUS. 346-399. One of the greatest masters of the spiritual life and of psychology in ancient monasticism; but his theological and philosophical speculation led him into wild heresy, which incurred condemnation at successive Church councils. His ascetic writings have continued to enjoy great authority. See the excellent edition of his *Practicus* by Antoine and Claire Guillaumont (Sources Chrétiennes 170), with a full introduction; also the ET of the *Practicus* and the treatise on Prayer by J. E. Bamberger (Cistercian Studies 4).

FABER, Father F. W. 1814-1863. One of the leading English converts to Catholicism in the 19th century; founder of the Brompton Oratory. He was a prolific writer, with considerable theological and spiritual good sense. Some of his hymns have become classics.

FRANCIS of ASSISI, St. A favourite among saints. 1182-1226. He was filled with a romantic love of poverty, which he called his "Lady"; he received in his body the marks of our Lord's Passion.

GREGORY the GREAT, St. c. 540-604, Pope from 590. One of the greatest of early Latin spiritual writers and monastic theologians.

GREGORY of SINAI, St. A Greek monastic spiritual writer. Died 1346.

GREGORY THAUMATURGUS, St. c.213-c.270. He studied under Origen, and his Panegyric to Origen gives us a vivid picture of the great master's attractiveness and methods.

GRIMLAC. The author of a rule for solitaries, about whom nothing is known. He lived in the 10th century.

GUERRIC of IGNY. Cistercian writer. He became abbot of Igny in 1138.

GUIGO I, Bl. The great compiler of Carthusian legislation, and author of some remarkable Meditations. He became Prior of the Grande Chartreuse in 1109.

GUIGO II. Died c. 1193. Also a Carthusian. His *Scala Claustralium* was one of the most popular spiritual books in the middle ages, and circulated in various forms, ascribed to various authors. It was translated into English by an unknown spiritual writer of considerable merit himself.

GUILLERAND, Augustin. A modern Carthusian spiritual writer.

HERMAS. 2nd century Roman Christian, author of some very extraordinary and important writings, gathered together under the name of The Shepherd, which at one time was treated as being on a level with canonical scripture. He lets us see something of the everyday Christianity of his time.

HUGH of ST VICTOR. Died 1142. A Canon of St-Victor in Paris, a prolific writer of every kind of book.

HUMBERT of ROMANS, Bl. In 1254 he became the Fifth Master General of the Dominicans.

IGNATIUS of ANTIOCH, St. One of the early Christian martyrs (c. 107), and author of some of the finest early Christian writings, in which his fervent faith and love of God is expressed and his passionate concern for the unity and well-being of the Church.

IGNATIUS of LOYOLA, St. c. 1491-1556. Founder of the Jesuits, and author of the well-known Spiritual Exercises, which became one of the most popular spiritual classics of the western Church, and was even adapted in Greek by Nicodemus of the Holy Mountain.

IRENAEUS of LYONS, St. Bishop of Lyons and the first major post-biblical theologian of the Church. c.130-c.200.

JOHANNAN of EPHESUS. Died 586. Important Syrian church historian, and a leader in the Monophysite Church.

JOHN of ST THOMAS. Spanish Dominican. 1589-1644. He devoted himself to theology, and especially the theology of St Thomas Aquinas.

JOHN of THE CROSS, St. 1542-1591. The mystical doctor of the Church.

JORDAN of SAXONY, Bl. St Dominic's successor as Master General of the Dominicans; his correspondence with Bl. Diana d'Andalò, a Dominican nun and his spiritual daughter, is a treasure of medieval spirituality and a classic instance of spiritual friendship. He died in a shipwreck in 1237. Gerald Vann translated his letters in To Heaven with Diana! (London, 1960).

JULIAN of NORWICH. A lady recluse; one of the most attractive of the English mystics. c. 1342-1413.

LACTANTIUS. c.240-c.320. Christian apologist.

LEGENDA AUREA. The most successful of all medieval collections of lives of the saints, it was compiled by the Dominican James of Voragine, archbishop of Genoa (c. 1230-c. 1298).

MAILLY, JEAN de. Another Dominican compiler of lives of the saints; the first edition of his collection dates from about 1225.

MALLEUS MALEFICARUM. This became the standard textbook on witchcraft in the later middle ages and into the 17th century. It was written in 1486 by two Dominicans. It contains some interesting and important observations, and is not without compassion, even though it was written chiefly for the use of Inquisitors.

MORE, GERTRUDE Dame. Benedictine nun, directed by Augustine Baker.

NICEPHORUS. A Byzantine spiritual writer, of whom little survives and less is known. He wrote one of the most important treatises on the Jesus Prayer.

ORIGEN. A theologian and exegete, who left a deep impression on all subsequent theology, although some of his own teachings were later recognised as false. c.185-c.254.

PERALDUS, WILLIAM. A Dominican preacher and moralist, extremely well-known and popular throughout the later middle ages, but now almost entirely unknown. c. 1200-1271. The best introduction to him is by Antoine Dondaine, in *Archivum Fratrum Praedicatorum* 18 (1948), pp. 162ff. His writings are of considerable interest, as a witness to a pure Latin catholicism, as yet uninfluenced by the new thought of the Universities of his time.

PEREGRINATIO AETHERIAE. A late fourth century account of the pilgrimage of a Spanish lady abbess in the Holy Land and round about. It makes fascinating reading.

PHILOKALIA. An anthology of traditional monastic and ascetic writings, compiled on Mount Athos in the 18th century, and soon translated into Slavonic, and later into Russian. Selections from the Russian are available in English in Kadloubovsky and Palmer: *Prayer of the Heart* (1951); *Early Fathers from the Philokalia* (1954). A complete ET from the Greek is in preparation.

POLYCARP, St. Martyred for the faith c. 155. The account of his martyrdom, by an eyewitness, is of great value and interest.

REGULA MAGISTRI. One of the oldest Latin monastic rules.

ROLLE, RICHARD. c. 1300-1349. One of the more exuberant and enthusiastic of the English mystics.

SEVERUS of ANTIOCH. c. 465-538. Monophysite Patriarch of Antioch, and one of the great theologians of his period.

SOLOMON, ODES OF. An exceptionally beautiful collection of early Christian poetry, from the first or second century. A new edition with ET has recently been published by J. H. Charlesworth (O.U.P. 1973).

SOTO, DOMINGO de. 1494-1560. One of the great Dominican scholastic theologians of Salamanca, who played an important part in many of the great theological controversies of his day. He was one of the theologians who defended the rights of the Indians in the newly discovered lands of America and the West Indies; he also took part in the controversy with the Illuminati. He was one of the Imperial theologians at the Council of Trent.

SYMEON (Pseudo—). Author of an important Byzantine treatise on the Jesus Prayer. It is certainly not by the great mystic Symeon the New Theologian, with whose ideas it is in places incompatible.

THEODORE THE STUDITE, St. 759-826. A great Byzantine monastic reformer.

THOMAS AQUINAS, St. c. 1225-1274. The greatest Dominican theologian, regarded for long as the patron of all catholic theology. Although he was capable of great intellectual abstraction, he was always a great man of prayer. His vision of life is humane and comprehensive. In the "new" language of the schools, he was able to restate the traditional faith, and the traditional understanding of the Christian life.

THOMAS A KEMPIS. c. 1380-1471. Author of the very popular Imitation of Christ.

VINCENT FERRER, St. Spanish Dominican, one of the most famous preachers and wonderworkers of his day. c. 1350-1419. His Treatise on the Spiritual Life, written for Dominican novices, enjoyed a certain popularity; it is available in a rather unwieldy ET (London, 1957).

WAY OF A PILGRIM. A very attractive little book of Russian spirituality, which drew the attention of Christians both east and west to the Jesus Prayer, leading to a great renewal of interest in the so-called "hesychastic" movement of prayer.

WILLIAM of ST THIERRY. c. 1085-1148. A Benedictine
monk who became a Cistercian, under the influence of his
friend St Bernard. He was one of the more intellectual and
reflective Cistercians, but his writings breathe the same spirit
of devotion and personal relationship with Christ. His most
famous and widely read book is his Golden Epistle, or Letter
to the Brethren of Mont-Dieu, which is a résumé of monastic,
spiritual doctrine.